# CHINNOCK

## *A BUTLER'S STORY*

WILFRED CHINNOCK

# CHINNOCK

## *A BUTLER'S STORY*

ꕥ

WILFRED
CHINNOCK

*PJE Productions*

ISBN 978-0-9565689-0-8

First published in Great Britain in 2010 by
PJE Productions
28 Carters Way, Wisborough Green, West Sussex RH14 0BY
email: peter.j.edmonds@btinternet.com

Reprinted March 2011



A CIP catalogue record of this book
can be obtained from the British Library.

Book printed by
THE ELLIOTT GROUP
Alchorne Place
Portsmouth
Hampshire
PO3 SQL

ꕥ

# CONTENTS

ജ്ര

# ILLUSTRATIONS

ꝏ

# EDITOR'S FOREWORD

**WHEN MY FATHER-IN-LAW** asked me to read the draft of his book in 1980, I was concerned, at first, about the style of his writing but said nothing to him. As I got into the atmosphere of the content, I realised that the mixture of expression, syntax and vocabulary was a reflection of his soft Somerset brogue and the adoption of words and phrases common in his working environment.

He was a great raconteur and had so often related to us, his family, many of the stories he had now recorded in this book. There were many others too, like the one of how his mother sent him a shoebox of primroses in the spring to remind him of the Somerset countryside.

I began to build a picture of the man, and his life in the years long before I knew him. Here was a young man, plunged into a world he could not even have dreamed of, who gives us now a glimpse of history from his perspective. I have entered into a journey of discovery during my research of this book helped along by the author's colourful descriptions of life in the 1930s.

I have edited punctuation and have broken up long sentences and paragraphs to make reading easier. However, I have not attempted to correct anomalies and inconsistencies. I have researched historical facts and names and, where there are inaccuracies, I have made corrections if I have been able to establish the truth. For this latter purpose I have used footnotes where it would be difficult to change the original text.

Otherwise, I have left the text exactly as the author intended with one exception: I have moved the final chapter, originally headed 'Conclusion', and included it as part of the Author's Foreword. It seems to be more comfortable there. In its place, I have divided the last chapter into 'The Last Months' and 'Epilogue'.

*Peter Edmonds*

ཀོ ༄

# AUTHOR'S FOREWORD

**THE PART OF MY LIFE** that touched upon that of my employer, Harold Sidney Harmsworth, Viscount Rothermere, seeks to show the man as I knew him. With the controversies of his life, I had little to do.

I have endeavoured to write chiefly of the man who was to me great and beloved, and to all who knew him, I believe, a very remarkable man and patriot who rendered invaluable services to his country and to whom I was honoured to be a devoted servant.

I had never thought to write my own memoirs until after I had retired two years ago, when I was invited to a party with my wife at our daughter's house in Wisborough Green. There were about thirty guests present. During the evening a conversation arose which centred on Fleet Street, and it transpired that one of the guests worked on the *Daily Mail.* I was able to air my views about a number of newspaper people, we sat and gossiped, and that was that.

A day or so later, however, my daughter, Hilary, received a letter from one Allen Synge who was preparing a book for publication. It was to be called *The Supreme Servant, a Celebration of the British Butler.*[1] The book was to have an introduction by Lord Carnarvon, with contributions from the Duchess of Devonshire, and there would be a series of interviews with famous butlers. The letter read:

> ***"I hear from my mother that your father may have some interesting experiences to recount. I hope this is correct and if so would he be prepared to be interviewed for the book?"***

This information being passed on to me, an interview was arranged, and took place at a later date, when Mr.Synge brought his mother to

1 The book was never published

tea at our house in Bognor Regis. We all enjoyed the interview, and when he had taken all the notes that he might require, he turned to me and said, "My goodness, you have had a most interesting life, have you never thought to write a book yourself?"

"Well yes," I said, "I had." but added that there was such a thing as libel which I did not understand and that I might be on dangerous ground.

"Oh no," he told me, "you write your story in the first person, and as long as you write it with no defamatory statements about anyone, I'm sure you can write a very interesting book that people would enjoy reading."

So, having taken his advice, I trust that my readers may enjoy my memoirs.

*Wilfred George Chinnock*

# Chapter I

# THE BOY

**MY NAME** is Wilfred George Chinnock. I was born at Cogley House, Bruton, Somersetshire in 1912; the eighth child of a family of nine. I went to a Church of England school in Bruton, and at the age of 14 was glad to leave; I don't think I learned very much at school. And so to work.

I began in a local bakery shop on a one-week's trial – and one week it was. My first job each morning was to take a halter and to walk a half-mile to fetch the horse. He was an angry brute and kicked somewhat, and I, being a small boy, was very frightened. Therefore, after a frustrating week with the horse and the smell of yeast in the bakehouse, where I was being taught to knead dough, I was thankful to leave my first post.

On the following Monday morning came a message from my schoolmaster. I must go and see him as soon as possible. I had visions of having to go back to school for another term. I did not want that to happen as I just hated the very thought of school. On my way to keep the appointment, I was thinking hard how I could get out of such a disagreeable situation. What could he be wanting to see me for, if not to tell me that I must come back to school again?

I duly reported to the classroom and awaited my fate. "Chinnock," said the Headmaster "how would you like to have a job in London?" My spirits rose immediately. In my present mood, Timbuktu would not have been too far to escape another term at school. So I said, "Yes." at once.

"Well now," said the Headmaster, "you must think this over thoroughly and go home and get your parents' permission. If they agree, I want you to go and see Mr A.T.Powlett, a gentleman farmer who lives nearby, and he will tell you more about this London job."

Telling my parents first, and not understanding in the least the hardship they would have in kitting me out with clothes etc., I prevailed upon them to allow me to go for an interview with Mr A.T.Powlett. He was a very kindly man, with a great scar on one cheek, who invited me into his study. "Well yes, you look a very likely lad," he said, "but are you sure you understand fully. London is a long way away from home; have you thought of that?" Yes, I had, and was undaunted. "Well, the situation is this: you see, I happen to belong to a Gentlemen's Club in the West End of London. It is an exclusive club and is called *The Windham*. I have been asked if I could recommend a young man, such as yourself, to be trained in gentlemen's service. How does that appeal to you, do you think you would like to try?" Yes, I was sure I would.

"You must go back to your parents, then, and make doubly sure that you can accept this situation, then come back and acquaint me with the answer."

My parents, I know, were pleased for me and talked it over for a considerable time, asking if I was really sure that I wanted to go to London. After receiving the best advice in the world from my parents, I decided I did want this.

So, in due course, I re-visited Mr Powlett for further talks and he said he had no hesitation in recommending me, but if I undertook to take this situation I must stick at it as I would be letting him down if, after a couple of weeks, I became homesick and returned home. I had to convince him that I was made of sterner stuff than that! Then, with his blessing, a date was eventually arranged and there was to be no turning back.

My parents had also fully agreed, in spite of the fact that they had to purchase a suitcase and all the necessary clothing – a new suit, underclothes, handkerchiefs, socks etc. I mention this because it was the first time in my life that I had had so many clothes all at once, and I had never had more than one shilling in my hand.

The suitcase was one of the first purchases. I insisted it must be a nice one because a young lady, who lived nearby and went to high school, had promised to emboss my initials on it. I was delighted with this idea; but when, after quite a lot of expert effort, she came down the garden with a downcast expression and my suitcase – with the initials most beautifully embossed, upside down – there was nothing to do but laugh. She was very sorry, of course, but what was done could not be undone, and I said, "Well, it looks great when the case is lying down."

My next step was to pack, and when all the purchases had been checked, my case was eventually packed and ready for the great day. By now, I was beginning to realise the import of what I was doing, and got that little sinking feeling in my tummy.

It was arranged that I would be met at Paddington Station by a young lady, Hilda, who lived close by, and who was in a situation in Kensington Palace Gardens. So, with the local boys and girls watching my departure with my mother and father, we eventually arrived at Bruton Station with 114 miles to go to London town. My father gave me a £1 note and made me go and purchase my ticket – my first really responsible act. The single ticket to Paddington cost fourteen shillings so, with the six shillings left, I returned to my father who, when I offered the change said, "You keep that, my son, and put it in your pocket."

How rich I felt – it was the largest amount of money I had ever had, and I was looking forward to a new job in London with a grand salary of £24 per annum, to be paid monthly!

I thanked my father and by now, the train was coming into the station. I kissed my mother and father, with tears I wasn't brave enough to keep back, and that was the only time I saw my father cry. My mother's handkerchief had been discreetly used for quite some time.

So there I was, on my way to my great adventure, with six shillings in my pocket and a stamped postcard, which I would post when I reached my destination, to say that I had arrived safely.

After about thirty or more miles I became dry-eyed at last, and pretended to look forward to what lay ahead for me – endeavouring to remember the names of the stations on my journey because, up until now, thirty miles was the furthest I had travelled from home.

I had left my younger brother my collection of birds' eggs, which amounted to about eighty different species, and wondered, on my way to London, how they would survive in his care. The countryside had always been my great love, but I must keep my mind on more serious things now.

Mrs Chinnock
No 4 Lusty
Bruton
Somerset

The Postcard Home

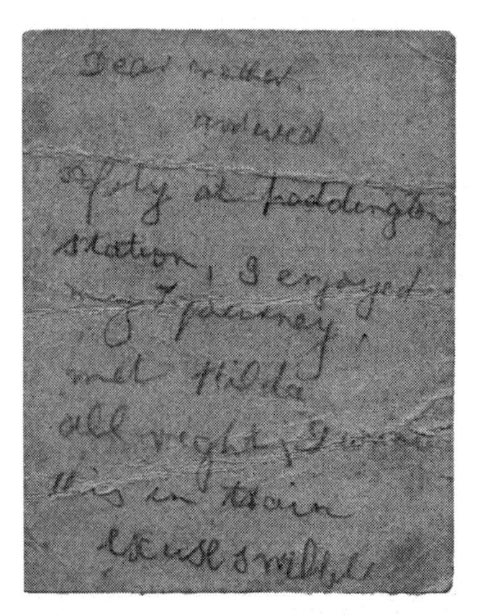

Dear Mother,
Arrived safely
at Paddington Station.
I enjoyed my journey.
Met Hilda all right.
I wrote this in train
excuse scribble.

## Chapter II

# THE BEGINNING OF THINGS

**ARRIVING AT PADDINGTON STATION** was a thrilling experience and I began to wonder how, with all these people about, my friend would be able to find me; but find me she did, and gave me a kiss of welcome – which I didn't really appreciate. Also, my ego was rather dampened because she took my suitcase and started off towards Praed Street to catch a bus which would eventually take us to Piccadilly Circus. However, I had to allow her to take charge for the time being and let events take their natural course.

At the end of Praed Street, we turned right into the Edgware Road. My companion was keeping me in touch, direction-wise, and as we neared Marble Arch, this was pointed out to me, then on through Oxford Street where Selfridge's enormous shop came into view. The populace of the metropolis was fascinating and I wondered where so many people came from. On to Oxford Circus and along Regent Street, then we arrived at Piccadilly Circus and from there, my friend told me, we must walk, so we alighted from the bus.

"So this is Piccadilly Circus," I told myself, and secretly I thought about Dick Whittington and his first impressions. Nothing like 'streets of gold', but wooden blocks, though at least I had never before seen streets made of such stuff.

We walked down Piccadilly a short way, then through Church Place and across an infamous street called Jermyn Street into Duke of York Street and so into St James's Square. Windham Club was No 13, and was in one corner of this green square, flanked by the London Library and, next door to that, The East India Club. We had to enter by the area steps and, on arrival at the door, we were greeted by the commissionaire, who asked us our business. We were eventually ushered into the steward's room where we were greeted by Mr Jones who was the steward at that time.

My friend had to take her leave as she had duties to perform in Kensington Palace Gardens. So, after making sure I had her address and telling me I could go to see her at any time, she took her leave.

The steward seemed a congenial kind of person, and after organising a meal, he made arrangements for me to see the housekeeper. My suitcase had already been dispatched to the luggage room and, after having eaten, I was taken on a short tour by the housekeeper, eventually being shown the dormitory where I would be sleeping. It was up about 80 to 100 steps – to the top of the building, and it was a large room with fourteen beds arranged around the sides. We then went back to the basement where I was allocated a locker and was issued with a key. My suitcase was produced and I stowed it away in the locker which was to be mine for the next five years.

It was now that I felt so all alone, as my duties did not commence until the next day. So I wandered around the dressing rooms and staff hall, speaking to various personnel who happened along. I learned that there were at least 60 staff members and most were in livery of some sort, undress livery, pageboy livery, valets and commissionaires.

At last, it was time for bed and this was where I met all the occupants of the fourteen beds. Putting on my very noticeable new pyjamas was, for me, an experience in itself, as I had never worn pyjamas before. Everyone seemed to settle down, most of the boys being about the same age or a little older than me, some from the country, but mostly cockney lads. Eventually it was 'lights out' and so, in the dimly lit dormitory – dimly lit because the lights of London were sufficient to give the room a glow – I crept out of my bed to say a prayer.

I was kneeling down and about to collect my thoughts when, from nowhere it seemed, I was showered with shoes, slippers and pillows, and there were howls of laughter from the dormitory as though they had witnessed an act of comedy. From that night henceforth, I said my little prayer in my bed, a habit which was to endure.

I experienced difficulty in getting off to sleep as the clock of St James's Palace, so close by, struck the hours, and it seemed I had just managed to drop off when the whole dormitory was rudely awakened. It was seven o'clock when the door opened and the janitor with a brass bell set the whole room echoing with its ringing. This was to be a daily routine which I would have to get used to in the future.

# Chapter III

# THE WINDHAM CLUB, ST JAMES'S

**FINDING MYSELF DOWNSTAIRS** and having yet to wash, as there were no washing facilities upstairs, I went to the dressing room and learned the 'drill' by watching what everyone else was doing. My locker was not far away, but it was a case of help yourself.

Someone told me to go to the stillroom and ask for Mrs Francis. On my arrival, and to my enquiry for that good lady, "Oh yes sonny," she said, "you have come for your ration." and forthwith furnished me with a half-pound of margarine and a bag of demerara sugar – this was to be a weekly issue to be kept in the locker.

Breakfast was available when we reached the staff hall. There was a pile of plates on which one of the kitchen staff doled out whatever happened to be on the menu. Tea was also served, sugarless; bread was placed at intervals down the table, to be used with the aforesaid ration – margarine and sugar. This meal was usually of one hour's duration, as staff duties varied and some people were always on duty, so when they had finished breakfast they took up their allotted tasks.

On reporting to the steward's office, I was furnished with a list of two foolscap sheets filled with commencement times and particulars of my daily tasks, which I was to learn by heart, and for the first two days, I was accompanied by a boy who knew the drill. My position was to be steward's room boy and I was to take charge of the messing arrangements of about six senior staff members. I had to learn what to get from the stillroom and what from the kitchen, which was a large stone-floored room at the other end of the building, where, I discovered, lived the chef, the pastry cooks, the vegetable cooks and roast cooks. I had to get all the necessary items from these departments to keep the steward's room supplied, so my list gave the times of meal times, of laying up, clearing and coping. The list seemed endless, but physically, things worked out quite well to the timetable, the secret being to know where everything came from. (All departments were situated in the basement).

This was to be my job for one month's duration and if I passed this test, I was told I would be allocated a livery.

There was, of course, a staff canteen, where small beer was on tap for staff who could afford to buy it.

This month was a very eventful one for me, for with so many youngsters, there was always trouble, and I always happened to be in the centre of it. I don't remember a whole week passing without being in a fight with one or other of them, but one lad in particular always picked on me and was delighted with his easy prey. One day, however, one of the more adult waiters said to me, "Aren't you tired of getting into scrapes?" I told him I was.

"Well son," he said, "you will never get any peace until you face up to that lad and give him a jolly good hiding."

Some time later, in the main dressing room, Tindale, for that was my tormentor's name, picked another quarrel with me. Quite a number of staff happened to be on the scene so they organised a circle around us and my champion grabbed both of us and said, "Alright you two, let's have a proper contest." and he let us loose like two fighting cocks. We began to fight and I looked after myself as best I could, and after about five minutes, which seem like an age, they separated us, both blood spattered and exhausted (at least I was).

Armistice had been declared with equal honours, and from that day henceforth, for the duration of my stay at the Windham, we were inseparable pals, and I never again had to suffer the indignity of being bullied by any other boy again – we were comrades in arms.

I had been writing quite frequently during this month, and wanting to go home, but of course, must wait until I had sufficient money.

My first pay-day eventually dawned and I found myself signing for £2. Great excitement was shown by all the youngsters on the staff and what they all seemed intent on doing was to get a Pontoon school started, into which I was initiated, but I must be careful not to lose my hard-earned wages. I became very skilled at cards, but sometimes I did lose my all.

My month's trial being up, I progressed from the stewards' room to start a new role – looking after the members. So, as I was to be a commis-waiter I needed an undress livery. I was therefore sent with a note to Woodrow's, the tailors, to be measured for a morning suit, which was made in a dark green material. Also an undress livery with tails, and trousers with a yellow stripe down each leg, and a wasp waistcoat with yellow and off-while stripes. The tailcoat, like a footman's, had link buttons of brass and brass side and tail buttons embossed with the letter W.

By the time this had all been attended to and after the usual fitting, I took possession of my livery and was told that if I looked after it and it was still in a good condition after one year, I could have a personal suit made to measure as a bonus.

Before I could dress myself in my new livery, I must first acquire a size fourteen butterfly collar and a cardboard dicky from Denny's in Little Pulteney Street,[2] the firm who supplied all the West End hotel and restaurant staff with such things. I bought myself two butterfly collars at 6d each and half a dozen cardboard dickies. I was advised to always have a few spare fronts because often when working under pressure the front button hole, which was attached to one's front stud, could, when the perspiring wearer least expected, be sliding down his chest; and as shirts were never worn, this could be quite embarrassing, to say the least.

As I was to be a commis waiter, I was told with whom I would be working. The waiter told me all I had to do, which was literally to fetch and carry for him and to observe the rituals of the dining room.

The dining room was very large, with close fitting very heavy carpets and with mahogany tables, mostly in singles all around the

2 Now part of Brewer Street

room. There was also a glass and wood area, partitioned off in the same room, and known as the *Strangers' Room*, where members could entertain their guests.

As one entered the dining room, there was a huge cold buffet table, with a chef always in attendance. There was a very good selection of the very best of meats, all garnished and looking very palatable, with nearly always a glazed boar's head as a centrepiece. The buffet itself was two-tiered with napery that reached to the floor.

The table linen was immaculate throughout the entire area and the serviettes were folded in 'bishop's mitre' fashion. I had, of course, been taught by now how to address any member who approached me and if he had a title, and I knew it, I must use it, but that it was the gentleman's prerogative to speak to me. In other words, I was only to speak if I was spoken to unless, of course, I was the bearer of a message – but even then, with decorum.

Two dumb waiters stood in suitable places, where the water jugs, rolls in baskets, crescent rolls and various other kinds of bread, biscuits, cheese, etc. were kept, in order to be get-at-able at any time when required.

Nearby sat the cashier at her desk, to settle accounts. She was rather a small person, and I had been told she was a Belgian refugee. She was very efficient and business like. Just across to her left hung a picture of *The Three Graces* – the only wall decoration in the dining room, and this was greatly admired.

The service doors were situated on either side of the buffet, with one-way traffic and brass kick plates, which led to the servery where the hot plates and bain-marie were situated, and just around the corner was a service lift to the kitchen and a blow-pipe to contact the kitchen porter who awaited orders from below.

I was feeling a little more settled now regarding my duties, but still very homesick. This was, however, offset by the thought that the summer holiday was just a couple of weeks away. How nice if I could hang on and arrive home with some grace. There would, of course, be lots to tell them. I thought of my first haircut in London and smiled to myself. Yes, they would enjoy that little story. At the time, it happened I was only aware of the fact that I must have a haircut, so off I went in search of a barber's shop. I soon found one at the top of York Street. Whereupon I entered and an assistant soon had my hair shaped and asked if I would like a little cream. "Yes please." I replied.

I now looked quite smart again.

"That will be 2/6d." said the man.

"I have only one shilling." I replied.

"Just a moment Sonny." and the owner of the establishment arrived on the scene. "Hello, what seems to be the trouble, where do you live young man?"

"I work at the Windham Club in St James's Square and I've only been in London a short time."

Where was my home, the man asked me, and I told him Bruton in Somerset.

"How much did you pay the hairdresser at home?" he next asked me.

"Thrupence." I told him.

"Well, laddie, I'll tell you what I'll do, my price is 2/6d but because you are new to London, give me 3d but don't come into my shop any more unless you are prepared to pay my price!"

I thanked him very much indeed, and I soon discovered that the class of barber that I needed in future, lived in Windmill Street, near Berwick Market.

The time flew by and I was soon on my way home on my holiday. The Club was to be closed for one month while the decorators did the necessary annual clean up. The staff had two weeks' holiday and on returning for duty, reported either to White's Club, or to Boodle's, whatever arrangement had been made. It was the done thing in London's Clubland that members became honorary members of another club whilst their own clubs were being decorated.

The talk among the waiters was that Boodle's was the favourite club to be chosen for, and if they were lucky enough to be so detailed, they were delighted because Boodle's was the only London club to have female staff in the dining room. So joining the Boodle's club for two weeks was a much sought after duty where the waitresses were known to be very smart indeed.

On the day my holiday commenced I sported 2/6d on a taxi to take me to Paddington Station. The weather was lovely, everything was in tune with my heart, and I willed the train to speed me back home.

What a homecoming, and what excitement! Everyone was pleased to see me and eager to hear of my experiences in London. The local girls and boys were keen to know what the latest tunes were, and would I hum a few of the latest hits, because of course, as yet, wireless was in its infancy, and the only way to get the latest tunes was to be where it all happened in London's theatreland.

Fortunately, at that time I had a harmonica so could keep them happy with snatches of the current hits from the shows, so, consequently, I was quite a popular figure and in great demand.

My mother said she thought it would be nice to call on Mr Powlett, as he would be sure to want to know the progress I had made, but I was secretly thinking I wouldn't return to London, so what would be the point? However, I was persuaded to go up to the farm and was at once invited in to tea and introduced to Mrs Powlett. They were very pleased to see me and told me how smart I looked, and that London would be the making of me. Mr Powlett told me he would be coming to the Club in a few weeks time, and as I took my leave, he pressed half a crown into my hand and said what a good lad I was.

My holiday was nearly over, the time had galloped past, and I didn't want to return to London. My parents said I should go just for a little while longer, that I would soon get used to it, and anyway what would Mr Powlett think if I didn't go? I wouldn't be able to look him in the eye again. I did return and somehow meeting all my workmates did put a different light on things, but it did not prevent my longing for home.

Getting back to routine was rather difficult, but I was soon in the swing again. Shortly after this, there was catastrophe – a General Strike! Things were happening in London – or rather not happening. Suddenly there were no buses, no trains, nor any kind of transport, and I felt completely cut off from home.

However, it's an ill wind that blows nobody any good, they say – the strike in itself was a terrible inconvenience, but by the time it was over, I knew the West End of London like the back of my hand. I had walked with the other lads and what one didn't know the other one did. We walked to Paddington Recreation Ground or Battersea Park and often to Regents Park, because of one our members was also a member of the London Zoological Society and often gave us free tickets to the Zoo.

I witnessed the supply of milk that was to keep London going, delivered to a huge depot in Hyde Park, then redirected from there. The strike proved a very interesting part of my life and I ceased to feel homesick, and felt I had grown up.

I was to see many interesting events in the future. For instance, I saw the taking up of the road through the whole length of Piccadilly, all the wooden blocks being piled high, and I believe lots of them were used as firewood. I also witnessed the rebuilding of Regent Street at the Piccadilly Circus end, and the rebuilding of part of Swan & Edgar's. Incidentally, I also saw the famous escapist, Houdini, hanging by his feet in a straight jacket, suspended from a crane at Swan & Edgar's, and his wonderful escape routine.

Also, whilst at the Windham Club, we boys had, of course, known the thrill of having a wireless crystal set with two sets of earphones. We threw our aerial out of the high window then endeavoured to get the *cat's whisker* to make a suitable connection with the crystal. When that happened, and it often did, we would hear: (at least four of us would) "This is 2LO calling and this is the Savoy Hotel Orpheans Dance Orchestra." Great excitement followed, some of the other lads crowding around the earphones to get in on the act. Then the *cat's whisker* would become dislodged and there would be silence, so the whole exercise would have to be repeated.

On one occasion, I went to Croydon Airport to welcome Colonel Charles Lindbergh, who, in the *Spirit of St Louis*, had been the first man to fly the Atlantic solo. I should have said I and about another million enthusiasts, because the crowd was so great that as the plane eventually came into sight it was impossible for the poor man to land on his first attempt and he had to circle once before he could land.

At the moment of landing, the vast crowd converged on the plane breaking supporting barriers on their way. Personally, my feet weren't touching the ground and I suddenly found myself right next to the plane, in fact, I was pressing against the fuselage where crazy people were trying to tear bits off for souvenirs. That was one crowd I was glad to get out of safely, as the ambulance men were working overtime and many people were crushed under foot.

To return to the Windham Club, I must tell you that I eventually became a valet and got to know lots of members, among whom was an elderly gentleman named Sir James Agg-Gardner who was, I was told, the Grandfather of the House at the time.

Famous names and well-known people I was dealing with about this time included Mr Dudley Ward and Mr Hart Davis, popular society people at that time. Another interesting gentleman I was to meet was Mr Walter Monckton, later Sir Walter, and Mr F.T.Barrington Ward who, I believe, was a barrister at Thames Police Court. They were often in each other's company and, so I imagined, must be in the legal profession.

Sir Roderick Jones, Head of Reuters, was also spending quite a lot of time at the club. He was a most fastidious man and would have his suits freshly pressed each day. His shoes were polished completely – heels, soles, insteps, and his silk shoelaces were washed and ironed and, of course, he had a complete change of linen daily. Two bottles of Contrexéville water were always to be available at his bedside.

Learning to be a valet was a hard task, where punctuality was a moment before and not a moment after. A list of members was kept in the valets' room, with bedroom numbers, times for calling, duration of stay, tea (whether China or Indian), apple, orange or whatever.

There were three floors of bedrooms containing about thirty beds, and along the corridors were personal lockers where some members kept their London clothes. There was a mahogany letdown table on each landing for brushing clothes, and on each half landing the toilets and baths were situated.

At the time I am writing about there were no hand-basins with running water in the bedrooms, and therefore the hot water had to be taken to each bedroom in water cans and placed in the wash stand bowls after removing the cold water jug and placing it beside the stand, a towel being placed over the hot water can to keep the warmth in.

Running the valets' department was the head valet, first and second valets and boots boy. I eventually rose from boots boy to first valet. As boots boy, I had to clean all the boots and shoes and also bring from the stillroom all the early morning calling equipment: tea pots, milk jugs, hot water jugs and 'screws' of tea – white for Indian, blue for China. To explain this – a measure of tea was wrapped up in a screw of paper and placed in each teapot; if it was Indian tea it was white paper and if China tea blue paper was used.

The information as to our requirements was communicated to the stillroom each day. We did have internal Metrophones, as we then called them, between the various departments.

It was also my job to get the newspapers each morning at 6.30 a.m. So, after consulting the list, I went to the St James's Theatre in King Street, just across the square, where I would find the newspaperman who used the steps of the theatre to display his newspapers. *'The Pink-un'*[3], I remember, was quite popular at the time and I always had one on my list, but the *Financial Times*, the *Times* and the *Daily Telegraph* seemed to be the usual trend. Having safely got the papers back to the valets' room, they were marked off for the rooms where they were eventually distributed with the morning trays.

I now commenced my shoe cleaning. There was a long narrow bench in the valets' room where all the boots and shoes were waiting to be cleaned; I having previously collected them from the three floors above and also having chalked the bedroom numbers on the soles so that I could return them to the correct bedrooms. There were about thirty pairs to be cleaned, and there would be another thirty pairs to be cleaned later. The ones on the bench were the evening shoes, the day shoes having already been dealt with the previous evening.

3 The nick-name of *The Sporting Times*

Our shoe cleaning equipment had to be kept to a very high standard, and the brushes and leathers (chamois) regularly washed in soapy water. Some gentlemen wore blacking leather boots, which called for special treatment with liquid blacking, which was applied after all surfaces had been thoroughly cleaned with soap and hot water. They were then 'boned' to get all the creases out and finally the chamois leather finished off a good job.

I remember that on one occasion a Mr H.C.Fowler who occupied No 15 bedroom and who was a regular rider in Rotten Row, had left his riding boots to be cleaned. On my way downstairs with the boots, I had passed the head valet, who was in conversation with one of the members on the middle landing. Ten minutes later, having cleaned the boots, I was returning with them. When I got to the middle landing, the head valet, on seeing me asked, "Where are you taking those riding boots laddie?"

"Mr Fowler's room, Sir."

"Take them back to the valets' room and I will be with you shortly." On his arrival he said, "Take your coat off lad and get some nice soapy water in that sink." and he picked up the riding boots, complete with trees inside and dropped them both into the sink. "Give them a jolly good scrub lad."

I scrubbed them for ten minutes before drying them off. At this point he said, "Not good enough!" and returned them into the water again with instructions to scrub them some more. Inside I was indignant and rebellious, but continued to scrub.

"That's enough, now dry them thoroughly. Now you can apply the blacking; now bone them and bone them again; now leather them and leather them again." he said. By the time my task was over, the riding boots gleamed with a glass-like surface.

"That's more like London, isn't it my lad? You can take them upstairs now and watch how you carry them or you will spoil your good work."

By now I was seething – I had been employed for two hours on one pair of boots and I was near to tears. Having delivered the boots I returned to the valets' room, and I must have looked a picture of dejection, for the head valet came and put his arm round my shoulders and said "You're a good lad, you acquitted yourself very well and I am proud of you, and I know and you know, that you will never forget how to clean a pair of riding boots."

One day the head valet asked, "Have you any money in the Post Office Savings Bank, because it's time you started to save some of your money." I told him I had not as yet had enough money to save.

"How much money do you happen to have on you?"

I told him I had £4.10s.0d. and I had now produced my pocket book for him to see.

"I'll tell you what I'll do laddie," he said, "I'll take your £4.10s.0d. in exchange for this," – and he produced a nicely folded brand new £5 note, white and crisp – "but only on condition that you go at once to Church Place Post Office and open a bank account."

What a surprise! I'd never had a £5 note in my life, so I readily agreed. I ran up Duke of York Street to Church Place like a dog and into the post office.

"Yes sonny, what can I do for you?" said the official.

"I would like to open a post office savings account please." and I then produced a brand new £5 note.

"Where did you get this from my lad?" said the man, who by now had two more assistants scrutinising my fiver and me. So I told them my story, and was quite relieved when he accepted it, but told me to write my signature on the note. This was then exchanged for my first post office savings book, but at the same time I did feel a little like a thief who had been caught with his hand in the till.

Soon after this, I stepped into the position of second valet and was taught the rudiments of valeting. How to go into a gentleman's room in the morning, how to draw the curtains with the least noise possible. How to collect and deal with the clothes sometimes strewn about the room, how to fold and leave them neatly, and how never to make a noise with the early morning tea tray and how, on leaving the room, to take the suit and shoes. It was possible the suit would be required again so it must be brushed and returned to the wardrobe.

Learning about the individual gentleman is what valeting is all about. Some will have a complete change of fresh linen twice daily and it is up to the valet to find out who's who, by looking at the luggage and the fashion of the packing; by the trade mark in the clothes – all good tailors leave their labels on the inside of the inside pocket, in the back seam of the trousers, and the back of the waistcoat belting.

The best shoes and shirts usually came from Jermyn Street, Bond Street, Saville Row and Cork Street and were very expensive. When one was in a position to examine the clothes and personal effects such as cuff links, dress studs and other personal jewellery it was easier to understand the kind of man with whom one was dealing – and some were simply fabulous.

The drill for receiving a gentleman into his room was to unpack his luggage and to arrange everything in correct order on the dressing table and in the wardrobes and cupboards and in the drawers etc., dress clothes being kept separate from day wear. Some people brought quite a lot of clothes, others not so many – depending, of course, on the duration of their stay. Some members might stay for just one night; it depended on their business.

By 6 p.m., the member's clothes must be laid out. If he had a dinner jacket *and* tails, both had to be laid out on the bed in readiness. The evening shirt had to be studded and the cuff links put in. Many members had matching links and studs for full evening dress and the appropriate ones had to be found in the necessary jewellery box.

Most shirts were starched and some links were therefore difficult to get through the buttonholes, and until one was really proficient, the use of a linen handkerchief to force the issue, was desirable, in order not to spoil a clean cuff. The front studs varied, of course, some were solid and these were pushed through the lower part of the front only, others unscrewed in the middle and were thus separated, the base being put into the lower part of the shirt front, and the tops, which were often diamonds, gold, or platinum, were placed on a folded handkerchief on the dressing table, beside which would be a white tie and a black tie and a starched collar.

Every detail had to be catered for, even to the comb which had to be placed coarse side uppermost between the hairbrushes. The shoes were placed beside the bed chair, the laces being loosened and the tongue pulled right back and a shoehorn laid across them.

Having completed my ten rooms on one landing, and checked every detail, ready for the head valet's inspection, there was then a waiting period until about 8 o'clock, by which time anyone dressing would have vacated their rooms. The day clothes were then brushed and put away. Some members would not change at all, so their evening clothes were put away again, but whether or not the member chose to dress, his clothes were laid out each evening, religiously, for the duration of his stay. Nothing was left to chance or taken for granted.

One American gentleman, I remember, always wore pure silk shirts heavily pleated for daywear; he had dozens in his wardrobe and changed them daily, the soiled ones being sent out to be dry-cleaned at the French cleaners at 3/6d each. My weekly wage of 10/- was dwarfed in my thoughts. Looking back it is difficult to imagine how such opulence was possible. Eton and Harrow, The London Season, The Grey Toppers and Morning Clothes, Ascot, Lords and all the other functions, the Garden Parties at the Palace, the fine jewellery and trappings that went with all these special occasions.

I became first valet and learned how to iron silk hats, sponge and press suits and generally to take things as they came. By the time I reached my eighteenth birthday, I had already dressed my first gentleman for St James's Levy. He was a very tall man, Robert Boothby. His tin boxes having arrived from the military tailor, I unpacked them and then had the special task of assembling the cockade in the hat and preparing the military sword and boots. After a somewhat hectic half-hour, headway was made. The high boots were made to fit inside the red striped trousers, which fastened under the instep of the boots. At last, fully arrayed and looking very splendid, the sword was arranged and last of all the magnificent headwear.

"How do I look?" asked Mr Robert Boothby.

"Immaculate, Sir Robert." I replied.

"You are a little previous aren't you?" he said, "I haven't been dubbed yet." I eventually called a taxi – though it was only a short trip to St James's Palace; and he was on his way to the investiture, leaving me with a nice smile and a handsome tip for my efforts. This gentleman's son was later to become a life peer and is now Lord Boothby.

At this time the Windham Club was having its centenary dinner and many of the distinguished gentlemen attended, including I remember – Mr Ramsay Macdonald, F.E.Smith, Lord Birkenhead and lots of others.

Clubland was a very friendly place and I met all kinds of sporting people. Most London clubs had their own football or cricket teams. The Army & Navy and the Royal Thames Yacht Club had very good teams. I played cricket for our club and had most enjoyable games. Once every year the staff played the members and on these occasions our Mr W.H.Whitbread, who was a member, would invite us all to his estate near Hitchen in Hertfordshire, where everything was laid on for a very memorable day's cricket, and sometimes the members won – nothing like keeping them happy! We usually set off from St James's Square in a charabanc well stocked with food and liquid refreshments, and ladies were allowed to join in for the day's outing. After the cricket match, we enjoyed our refreshments and later in the evening we were invited to the local fete, which always seemed to take place on the same day, so playing the members was a red-letter day for us.

Whilst I was at the Windham Club a cousin of mine, who was known in the theatre as Violet Gaynor, was booked to appear at the Plaza. Most cinemas at that time always contrived to have quite a grand interlude between the films. Sometimes it would be Billy Cotton's band, who would entertain for about half an hour, but on this occasion, it was to be my cousin who was to sing *So Blue*, a current hit. So, of course, I told all the lads at the club that my cousin was on at the Plaza. Most of them decided that I was leg-pulling, but a few of us did go and we witnessed her performance – in a completely blue setting – I felt very proud, but never knew how many of my Windham Club contemporaries really believed that she was my cousin. Incidentally, she ended her days living with Billie Russell the comedian, at Reading.

There was always a Christmas list to which the members subscribed for the benefit of the staff, each year. Also, we had an annual staff dance to which some members came. So the morning room had to be cleared of furniture, and suitable arrangements made for the dancers' convenience. Many hands made light work and it took but a short time to transform the morning room into a grand dance salon. Invitation tickets were necessary to gain admission and all the staff were allowed to have guests, small engagement dance programmes with pencil attached were received, so that dances could be booked in advance.

London during the two years – 1929 to 1931 – was a very interesting place to be. The Alhambra, Leicester Square, was still a popular place of amusement, with Billy Bennett in *Almost a Gentleman*. Norman Long the pianist, Nellie Wallace and Wee Georgie Wood were still going strong. I also witnessed, around that time, an exhibition-boxing bout on the Alhambra stage between George Carpentier and Primo Carnera. The talkies were on their way in: Al Jolson at the London Pavilion in *The Singing Fool* and its song *Sonny Boy* – a picture that was immensely popular.

The London Underground had opened the Piccadilly Circus station, which the workmen had been working on for years, and Eros reappeared after being absent from the London scene for quite some time. The London flower girls were back with their nosegays, and the London General Omnibus Company and the Brown Pirate Buses would soon be disappearing and the old London town would lose some more of its charm.

The airplane was seen much more often and Amy Johnson, Jim Mollison and Amelia Earhart were often in the news. The *Daily Mail* was often advertised in sky-writing above Piccadilly Circus. An interpreter could always be seen outside the Popular Cafe to help our foreign visitors on their way. Yes, London was the 'Hub of the Universe' where I was once told if one could wait long enough one would most certainly meet most of the people one ever knew. Personally, I became very fond of London and visited most places of interest.

I took particular pleasure in visiting Covent Garden in the early hours of the morning, or Middlesex Street – better known as Petticoat Lane, and I would often explore the City of London on a Sunday morning, when it became a deserted place. I would walk around its quiet streets and explore its secrets. Transport was quite a reasonable price. One could buy a shilling all-day ticket on the trams and I found I could cover an amazing distance during the day. Many times, I rose very early to see the London streets being cleaned and hosed down. No-one took any notice as the metropolis never sleeps, so they tell us. The poor down-and-outs could be seen scattered far and wide. The Embankment, or any likely spot, would find some poor soul asleep, all huddled up with brown paper or newspaper to keep them warm. They could sleep in the London parks during the day but at night all the parks were locked, so they slept on the pavements around Marble Arch or any convenient corner. Many times I saw these poor wretches scavenging around the West End hotels' swill bins – a very sorry sight.

Before I finish my experience at the Windham Club, I must, I think, relate a story against myself, which happened on a dismal winter's afternoon. I had washed a shirt and a few smalls and had them in a large enamel bowl to boil on a gas ring that stood in the valet's room at the end of the shoe- cleaning bench.

I was by myself and the fire looked dismal and as it was inclined to be chilly, I thought I would brighten the fire up a little, so I crossed to the valets' bench and picked up a bottle of cleaning fluid. That was my first mistake – I had only intended to put a little in the fire, but how was I to know that the flame that started within the fire would run up the liquid and leave me with a flaming bottle. I quickly withdrew my hand away from the fire and in so doing spilled a flaming trail underneath a long table, which stretched the length, almost, of the opposite side of the valets' room, underneath which were stacked piles of top hats.

Having caught the place alight I endeavoured to put the fire out and the first to come to hand was my bowl of washing, which, with frantic haste I threw on the fire underneath the table. I was successful in putting out the flames, but then for the aftermath. As I hurriedly mopped up the water – speed was of the utmost importance as somebody could arrive at any time – I realised that many of the hats were ruined and there would be hell to pay. However, I kept calm.

Suddenly realising how lucky I was to have a sink standing at the end of the table, my fertile brain conceived a plan, so I hurriedly stacked all the top hats, which were the worse for this experience, in the corner nearest the sink, and having reached this point without being discovered, I took a breather and recapped on the plan which had formed in my mind.

For the moment, order was restored and I was counting my lucky stars at not being discovered. The next part of my scheme was to be more subtle and needed a time lapse. I blocked the sink with tealeaves and tampered with the 'swan neck' under the sink to encourage the desired leak which gradually developed into a small seepage.

On a morning later in time, whilst we were having a cup of tea with the head valet, I was able to say, "Look sir, the sink is leaking and there is water under the bench."

"Get those hats out for Pete's sake," he yelled. I was quickly employed delving under the table – as were the other two valets – and pushing the hatboxes 'willy-nilly' all over the valets' room floor.

The end of the exercise was that about 20 hats had to be sent around to Jermyn Street to be re-blocked, some grey toppers, some silk toppers. My job was saved; for needs must when the devil drives and I most certainly would have been sacked if instead of water, the truth had leaked out.

## Chapter IV

# CHISLEHURST GOLF CLUB

TO CONTINUE with my career: I was in my nineteenth year and had quite recently met a charming young lady who happened to be employed in private service in Chislehurst, Kent, and having visited Chislehurst and finding that I liked it very much, I decided to throw my hat over the proverbial windmill and endeavour to get some kind of employment there. So, in due course, I succeeded in obtaining a situation at the Chislehurst Golf Club.

Changing jobs always had pitfalls, and as I was quite some distance from my home, I had to be self-sufficient and make sure I had enough money to subsist on in case things went wrong. There was no dole money or any other kind of financial aid in those days, so when I say I threw my hat over the windmill, you will gather my meaning. However, everything was satisfactory on this occasion and I had been able to arrange my notice at the Windham Club and commence my new duties within one week.

The Golf Club was housed in Camden House, Chislehurst, which stood in the centre of the common. It had historic connections and was once the home of the Princess Eugene, wife of Napoleon III of France, and standing nearby on the common was a statue of the Prince Imperial, her son, who was killed in action in the Zulu War. It was a charming building and, besides being a golf club, housed several permanent residents, amongst whom was Mr O.A.Critchley and his wife. He was the Secretary of the White City Greyhound Racing Association that had recently been formed and the father of Brigadier General Critchley, who married the ladies open golf champion, Joyce Wetherhead.

I liked the work, as it was relaxing after my London club experiences. I did a few valeting duties and also took part in the dining room service. Weekends were the busy times when members came in from the surrounding districts to play golf and often stayed over for lunch. I was also able to play golf myself, and after some time had my own set of clubs. We had quite a few well-known members, Rex and Lister Hartley were two such golfing brothers (from the famous jam family). I was happy too, in as much as I could get some courting in, between times, as my girl friend's place of residence was just the other side of the common. We arranged to get our leisure time off together. Her name was Rosemary and she hailed from Stone Crossing in Kent.

Staff at Camden House numbered twelve, extra staff being taken on for special functions. There were wedding receptions occasionally, also Masonic evenings, when the dining room was transformed. The checkered black and white carpet came out and the regalia of the Masons were arranged around the room. When all was ready, the Lodge members entered and all the doors were locked with the exception of one, outside which was stationed the Tyler who barred anyone's approach until such time as the meeting was over. These activities took place after dinner had been served, so there was much coming and going to get the dining room prepared, firstly for dinner and secondly for the Masonic meeting. However, order was soon restored and whilst the meeting commenced, the staff were busily engaged in the pantry dealing with piles of washing up of silver and crockery and the putting away, which usually took a period of one hour plus. Afterwards we retired to the staff hall for our own refreshments.

In another part of the building were sitting rooms and, of course, the bar, where our permanent members were catered for at all times, and staff could be summoned by bell push to any of these departments. Eventually the Masonic meeting would be ended and the Tyler would tell the staff. We could now commence the clearing of the Masonic furnishings which all had to be stowed away until the next Lodge meeting. The dining room furniture could be replaced, and the breakfast tables laid in readiness for our resident members. There were usually about ten permanent members, plus the Club Secretary who was a Major Ferguson at that time. During the week, there were always a number of chance luncheons and dinners. Weekends we were mostly fully booked, according to the weather. There was also a squash court, where the more athletic members could work up a real sweat, lose weight, and feel better for the exercise. Mr George Pike was the steward during my stay at the club, and he had his own private quarters where he lived with his wife.

There was, I remember, a bedroom, a circular room lined with green beige, and said to be haunted. The story being that at one time the gentleman of the house was foully murdered by his butler – seemed a likely story and so I mention it to the reader.

The next year or so passed very agreeably and I was able to play golf quite frequently. My girl friend and I took a weekly trip to London to keep up with the cinema and theatre. We could take a 2/6d. return ticket from Chislehurst to Charing Cross station, then wander around the West End; it was possible at that time to gain admittance to any West End cinema show before midday for the sum of 1/6d., which we were wont to do. Afterwards we would go to Lyons Popular Cafe, or the Coventry Street Corner House where we could get delightful 'Nippy' service in very agreeable surroundings, with an orchestra in attendance.

If we decided to visit the Coventry Street Corner House we could choose which floor to patronise, and as they each had their own particular orchestra in attendance it was always a pleasure which we very much enjoyed. I got to know the attendants in the cloakrooms quite well and there was always a special welcome and exchange of news when we met.

If we decided to go to the Popular Cafe, which was situated in Piccadilly, we could have a tea-dance and we often did. Popular it was called and popular it was, and just to sit and have tea and watch other young people dancing was a very enjoyable experience. The 'Nippy' waitresses to serve at table, too, was somehow quite elegant and appealed to a couple of sweethearts having a day out in London Town and, by the way, they served a mouth-watering compote of fruit with cream, which we often indulged in. We would then go on to find another show to see, maybe a theatre or another picture show, before ending our day's outing. We would then have a quick snack somewhere before returning to Charing Cross station, having enjoyed our day in town. As I settled into the corner seat, I would idly count the change in my pocket. We often had change from £1 and 25 shillings, at the most, was the total outlay for both of us, which, at the time of writing, seems almost ridiculous. Happy days!

My sister now enters my story, as she had just recently taken a situation in London, a very special one, as housekeeper to the Rt HonViscount Rothermere. This was to be the man on whom my future was to depend, in no small degree, and as my experiences unfold, you will understand.

But back to Chislehurst. Both my young lady and I were busily employed, but on future visits to London we often visited my sister, who was working for Lord Rothermere at 14 Stratton House, Piccadilly. We were very much impressed with what we saw and heard. Early in the year 1933, one of Lord Rothermere's secretaries made it known to my sister that a parlour maid was required at Stratten House. Whereupon Fletch – which was the nickname of my young lady, whose surname was Fletcher – was nominated for the position, and after the usual preliminaries she was accepted for the said post. I was, of course, delighted for her, but this left me in Kent and my sweetheart in London, and London was really where I wanted to be, so I had to engineer my future accordingly.

I had to have sufficient money to find digs in London and on my next trip to town, I made it my business to enquire for bed and breakfast. I was most fortunate, after searching around for a while, to discover, in Hasker Street, Chelsea, which lay behind Harrods in Knightsbridge, a lady who had just what I was looking for: a bed sitting room, with a morning cup of tea and two slices of bread and butter for six shillings per week. It was the answer to my prayer and I paid six shillings in advance because I would, of course, have to work a week's notice at Camden House before I could move in.

# Chapter V

# BACK TO LONDON

## The Bridge Club, Finchley Road

**AFTER A WEEK**, I duly returned to London and my little room in Hasker Street, Chelsea, and commenced to search for employment. In the meantime, I lived as frugally as possible. I knew a little Italian restaurant just off Piccadilly where I could buy very nice ham or salmon rolls at 2d. each and tea at 2d. a cup, and decided that I could get by on 6d. per day until I found employment, with the occasional fling when I met my young lady, when we would have something a little more substantial. In the meantime, I had to eke out my money.

Several weeks passed and I was getting a little desperate, when I received news of two Russian ladies who ran a Bridge and Poker Club in Finchley Road, North London. I arranged an interview and in due course met a Madam Polliakoff, one of the principals. There were drawbacks, the first that my duties would commence about 5 p.m. I would then be in attendance on her clientele throughout the night and early morning, and there was to be only one other staff member, but on the promise of the job being lucrative, and after meeting the partner who would help with the various duties, I agreed. One of the conditions was that both of us could supply full evening dress, tails and black tie. The condition having been overcome, we could start our duties. I remember the first evening as more of a comedy situation than a real one.

There was one large room on the ground floor with about ten bridge tables, and a large room on the first floor that housed two poker tables, and this appeared to be a club with a reasonable membership. In the hall were two fruit machines, one to play for shillings and the other for florins. The evening activities having started with quite a large party arriving and commencing to play bridge. Later on, as the members sorted themselves out, a poker table started. But first things first. One of the Russian ladies issued poker chips to all indulging in that particular game. The customers looked 'well-heeled' and some were very well dressed and quite a few were Russian Jews. The staff – that is my friend and I – hovered around looking important until some member decided to partake of refreshment, whereupon out would come the little bill pad and the order was written down with a flourish.

There then followed an elegant walk out towards the servery which, in this case, was in the basement. Once past the service door and a quick dash to the kitchen, off came my coat – and now to fulfill the order, plus Russian tea etc. Having completed the order: egg & chips, cutlets, steak, mushrooms, sausages, tomato was the menu, and placed it on a tray, I would quickly replace my coat and proceed back to the customer, looking as though I had casually gone to the servery to collect from the non-existent chef. My friend and I were tickled pink at our own antics, but as a few evenings went by we gradually coped with our double roles.

Lucrative it certainly was, we got many tips from the bridge playing members and when it came to the poker players they didn't bother with tips moneywise, but paid us out in chips, and if the recipient of some refreshment had had a recent good win a £1 chip came my way. After the evening's business was finished and the customers had all gone home, in the early hours, I often found I had quite a number of chips in 5/-, 10/- and £1, and my helpmate likewise. So, when the manageress had collected and checked the playing chips, they never agreed until she rang the bell or called us into her little office and exchanged our chips for cash. Her books would then balance and we could all go home – this was usually around 6 a.m. I would call a taxi to take me to the Cumberland Hotel at Marble Arch where I would partake of gammon rasher and eggs, toast and coffee for breakfast, before retiring to my little abode in Hasker Street, well satisfied with my night's work, but very tired too. As the weeks went I was amazed at the amount of money I was able to save, but the pace was to prove a bit too much, and I decided I didn't want to keep this job for too long, as I rather valued my health, but, for the moment, was content to make quite a bit of money.

The people who owned the fruit machines at the club, came once a week to empty them. On these occasions, the gentleman who performed this task would give me £3 from the one-shilling 'one armed bandit' and £5 from the two-shilling machine, and urged me to encourage customers to play. As it happened, they needed no encouragement, and I continued to get my little rake-off. I decided, however, that this was not the life for me, and after three months and many sleepless days, due to the fact that my next door neighbour in Hasker Street kept about ten blue Persian cats in her garden, who were at their noisiest during the day, I decided to leave.

Fletch and I became engaged on our 21st birthdays. We exchanged rings which we purchased at the Goldsmiths & Silversmiths Company in Oxford Circus. We looked at rings for a great length of time and I remember that our choice – a small cluster of diamonds cost 13 guineas, and my signet ring was £3. This seemed to us to be a pinnacle aimed for and reached. (I mention the price, not because I am mercenary, but because it now seems another world). We were very happy with and for each other. Saving money in those days seemed more like a campaign, and to buy a special gift one had to plan many months ahead, but the accomplishment was always most pleasant. I don't suppose for a moment that this was our own personal experience, every one of our contemporaries will know, and if they care to remember, cherish those days.

# Chapter VI

# I MEET ROTHERMERE

**FLETCH HAD BY NOW** worked for Viscount Rothermere for almost a year, and as I often went to Stratton House to see her, I met other members of the staff, including one of his stockbroker secretaries. He was a Mr F.J.Clark, who had been with His Lordship for many years, and was also a pal of Edward Fells, who had been His Lordship's valet for almost thirty years. They met frequently for weekends, and enjoyed the football season in London, not to mention cricket. A portable wireless was available I remember, a McMichael battery set which kept us in constant touch with the latest scores.

My sister, who was, at this time, cook-housekeeper, had decided to get married, and would consequently be leaving His Lordship's service. That meant staff reorganisation problems. Lord Rothermere had decided to use the Flat at Stratten House mainly for interviews, and the secretary asked me if it wouldn't be a good idea if I could come to work at the Flat. I could get married to Fletch, and we could run the place together.

The mere idea of a chance of this magnitude was beyond my expectation, and I simply jumped at it. It would, of course, mean that I would have to be interviewed by the 'Old Man' himself, as he was always affectionately referred to, though not within his hearing, naturally. At the appointed time, therefore, I was ushered into the great man's presence, a most remarkable man, whom, I felt, I must strain my wits to satisfy. A very stern looking man, out of the same mould as Mr Winston Churchill and Lord Beaverbrook – at least that was my impression. I was delighted to learn however, that the interview was successful. My wife and I were to receive a joint wage of £6 per week, though this was after asking quite a lot about my background.

£6 per week in 1935 seemed to be exceptional wages, and so it was. "When will you get married then Chinnock?"

He was way ahead of me, I hadn't thought about it.

"When is your sister Violet getting married?" he then asked.

"In two weeks' time, My Lord."

"Then you get married next week and pip her at the post." The interview was over. "Well, let me know what you decide to do." he said, "And, by the way, I like the way you looked me in the eye."

Everything happened so quickly, he wants to see Rose, as he calls my fiancée, and when he does, he says, "Why don't I get you a special licence? Then you can marry right away." But having set her heart on a church wedding, she told him so. "Do what you want to do my dear, but the sooner the better. It will take three weeks for the banns to be published. Alright then, I expect you both to be installed in the Flat in three weeks' time." And so we were. After three weeks we took up residence and then began some of the most exciting years of my life.

Harold Sydney Harmsworth, The Rt HonThe Viscount Rothermere P.C. of Hemsted in the County of Kent, to give him his full title, was indeed a most remarkable man at the time I entered his employ. One of the five richest men in England, a multi millionaire even after having lost £10,000,000 in the 1929 Wall Street crash. I learned that not only did he own two villas in the south of France, Villa Cap Martin and Villa Roc Fleur, but also Sunningdale House, Berkshire, St Dunstan's, Regents Park, London, Burghfield House, Dornoch, Sutherland, 79 Avenue Road, Swiss Cottage, London, Stody Lodge, Melton Constable, Norfolk, but also our own headquarters, 14 Stratton House, Piccadilly. This was most impressive. Also at this time, His Lordship's son The Hon Esmond Harmsworth owned Warwick House, St James's, where he lived with his family. This being his town house – his country seat was Merryworth Castle in Kent. As I got to know more about the great man I learned that he was also known as the Uncrowned King of Hungary, and was thought so highly of that millions of Hungarians petitioned His Lordship to accept the Crown of St Stephan, an elective crown which had never been offered to a Hungarian. This then was my boss and brother of Lord Northcliffe to boot. The Harmsworth family originated in Ireland where their father was a barrister and the two peers aforementioned were only two of a very large family, every one of whom was most distinguished in their own right. But my reader, if interested in the particulars of this family, could read Sir Max Pemberton's *Lord Northcliffe – a Memoir* which tells about Alfred Charles William Harmsworth – a story that began about 1879, and has little to do with my personal life story.

Here may I quote from Sir Max Pemberton's book to give the enormity of the combination of Rothermere and Northcliffe:

> ***"The scenery of Newfoundland is everywhere that of Scandinavia and, sometimes, greatly suggestive of Canada. Scotch firs abound and low tree-capped hills, such as we meet in Southern Norway and in Spain. There are immense herds of caribou in the Savanna country and, owing perhaps to this very fact, Lord Northcliffe came into possession of such tracts of land.***
>
> ***"In any case Lord Rothermere's and Sir Mayson Beeton's investigation confirmed the suitability of the island for one of their greatest enterprises. The company was quickly constituted and an agreement made with the Government of Newfoundland, by which was acquired on lease, a tract of country roughly 2,300 square miles in area with the water-power of Grand Falls and certain other valuable but smaller concessions.***
>
> ***The lease was for 198 years at a small annual rent, and in addition, the Newfoundland Government agreed to admit, duty free, all machinery and plant necessary to the construction and equipment of the paper mill."***

Maybe this will put my reader in the picture regarding the vast fortunes that were made by these two very astute personalities, but, of course, by the time I arrived on the scene, Viscount Northcliffe was already dead, and he left behind him a legend.

It was, I believe, in 1935 that Lord Rothermere decided to sell his house, St Dunstan's, which he had bought from the Otto Kahn the previous year. He had hoped to make its garden one of the finest in London and to do certain alterations to the house, but, as I understood it, it was Crown property and there were limitations on alterations in consequence. So, very soon, he sold it to the Woolworth Heiress Barbara Hutton who was, at that time, about to become Countess Reventlow.

He then concentrated more upon his house that was being completed at Stody. I was later to take up quarters there (in about a year's time) but in the meantime I had met the architect on several occasions, a Mr Walter Sarell and learned quite a lot about the house before we moved in. The heating was rather complicated being built on the ceiling panel system and quite 'with it'. It consisted of a series of copper panels built in, but on a try-out, I'm sorry to say, some of the ceilings fell down and caused a setback for a few more months, at some considerable cost to the contractors. Eventually all was well and the staff were able to move in.

At this time, Countess Reventlow had done her own thing. There was a fire at St Dunstan's, which did quite some damage, but afterwards she was able almost to rebuild the place completely. I, personally, never saw St Dunstan's,[4] but I believe it was a very special and beautiful place which, at this moment in time, is used by the Ambassadors of the United States of America.

Since the Flat was used, almost exclusively for interviews, I relished

---

4 Lord Rothermere was the last owner of St. Dunstan's when all that remained of the original interior was the "handsome elliptical entrance hall". In 1936 the house was partly destroyed by fire and it was bought by Barbara Hutton. Her friends suggested that St Dunstan's Villa might be an excellent site for the kind of home Barbara Hutton was seeking. Impressed by the peace and security of the grounds, she decided to buy and on 10th August 1936 the Crown Estate Commission gave permission for the old white stucco Regency villa to be pulled down and a red brick Georgian style house built in its place. This Winfield House is now the residence of the U.S. Ambassador to the United Kingdom.

my job most highly, never knowing which eminent personage I would announce to His Lordship. Mr Winston Churchill was a regular visitor and I think I met, almost certainly most of that decade of Cabinet Ministers. Harold MacMillan and Ramsay MacDonald were often visiting. There was also another MacMillan, a Captain Norman, who became President of the New League of Airmen that had recently been formed as part of a campaign Lord Rothermere had instigated in his fight to re-arm Britain.

I was interested in all the personalities – Sir Malcolm Campbell, George Lansbury and Francis Day. I met people from all walks of life and enjoyed having to receive them on His Lordship's behalf. On one occasion, when I opened the door, there stood the Regent of Hungary with three bodyguards. Herr Von Ribbentrop was Germany's Ambassador in London at this time and I often met his children with their Nanny in Green Park, which of course, was overlooked by 14 Stratton House, which was at the top and seventh storey of the building, where a most delightful view of the Park and Buckingham Palace could be observed.

All this was ours. My wife and I found much joy in being able to taste the fruits of luxury without actual cost, because when His Lordship wearied of his interviewing, he took himself off to Avenue Road, where a house full of staff took over to tend his slightest wish, whilst my wife and I had the whole flat to ourselves and we did, indeed, appreciate our lot.

Lord Rothermere was most kind and considerate in every way and I speak for all his servants when I say that they really loved him. I had often heard him remark that "My servants are the best friends I have." and I am sure he was right.

I did at certain times go to Avenue Road to do a dinner if he had a special party; actually I was 'on tap' any time really, as a 'phone call could have me chasing around to Avenue Road in a taxi with all the weekend reviews I could get my hands on. I could, for instance, receive a telephone call from his Secretary, Mr Jimmy Clark, on Monday with the message that His Lordship would be going to Scotland on Wednesday.

That meant that I must leave a day before him, so on Tuesday I must make my move. The Chef from Avenue Road would be required and maybe a parlourmaid and a couple of footmen from Norfolk. Usually there were about six people including myself. I would collect travelling expenses from the Secretary, book tickets and sleeping berths to Inverness. Having made arrangements I would make my way to Kings Cross station, where I would collect the staff who would, by now, have arrived and be waiting for me, collect the tickets and shepherd my little brood onto the 7.20 night train to Inverness. After stowing our luggage, we then met together in the buffet to partake of our evening meal and to talk together and share our news as we ate our way through a very pleasant meal with drinks suited to the individual taste. Anything within reason was an accepted code, and the tip I gave the car attendant was appropriate for services rendered and, of course, he knew perfectly well whose staff we were. Sometimes a false alarm would precede us to Inverness station and on one occasion the Stationmaster received us arrayed in full morning dress, having been alerted that His Lordship was on his way to Dornoch. It seemed that was the usual procedure, that he would greet His Lordship on arrival, but on this occasion he welcomed us the staff, and enquired when Lord Rothermere would be arriving.

It was always a most exciting experience; we would detrain at Inverness then wait for a connection that would take us to Bonar Bridge where we were met by car. We could, of course, have completed the journey to Dornoch by train but it usually took us an hour longer for the train to snake around the Firth, so we would settle for a car ride that would take us to Burghfield House much more quickly.

On arrival, we would sort ourselves out and unpack our cases etc. My next duty was to go and see a Mr John Sutherland who was the town clerk, who kept the combination of the strong room at the house in his private safe. After greeting each other and discussing the weather, he would produce an envelope with a heavy seal attached, which would then be opened to reveal the written combination of the strong room. Having taken possession and signed for same, I was then custodian until such time as we would close the house again on our return to London, when another visit to Mr John Sutherland would see the combination returned to its envelope and sealed again in each others presence, but beforehand he would have been with me at the moment when the strong room was locked.

Having the combination in my possession I would, by following instructions, be manipulating the safe dial, eventually pulling open a very heavy door behind which, in any man's language, lay a fortune in silver and jade and Cromwellian gold, Elizabethan silver and untold treasures, besides, of course, the great canteens of silver – dining room for the use of. It was my duty to arrange the art treasures around the house in their appropriate positions. Chinese jade and porcelain and the finest eggshell china, and to always keep my fingers crossed that no harm should come in the handling of such treasures. We had a skeleton staff at Burghfield, plus about five gardeners, who by now were producing the most amazing array of flowers to be arranged, and to be ready for the arrival of His Lordship, and we wondered who would be coming in his party this time.

I should, of course, explain now that all the art treasures had their own particular inventory numbers stamped upon them and that the man who kept tabs upon the whole of Lord Rothermere's art treasures and pictures in each of his establishments, including the two villas in the south of France, was a Mr Herbert Cescinsky whose headquarters were in London, and who was an authority on antiques and an accepted expert on such subjects. He gave two or three lectures each year in the United States of America.

I was in constant touch with this gentleman and got to know and respect him very much. If by chance His Lordship thought fit, and he often did, to present someone with any particular piece in the way of a gift, as he was a most generous man, the inventory number must be conveyed to Mr Herbert Cescinsky, the date of the gift noted, and the ultimate removal of that particular piece from his list of ownership, and to take off his list for insurance purposes. He must have had an enormous responsibility, as at Dornoch alone, the house contents could be valued at one million pounds, at least.

My story will now be found to jump from one place to another as my memory works the way it happened, and I shall often start a story at Burghfield House that might end at Stratton House or in Norfolk, and could appear to be rambling, but you will see how quickly I can be dispatched from one place to another at the drop of a hat.

I may as well tell you, whilst I am at Dornoch, that we had a private telephone line to London. We also had a private line from Norfolk to London, which meant that we could reach London, from either place, simply by picking up the telephone. A voice would answer, "This is Central 6000 – *Daily Mail*."

"Mayfair 3039 please."

and I could be talking to my wife quicker than I could 'phone the local golf club for caddie. At such progress, the mind boggles. Our morning papers would be delivered by plane landing on Dornoch golf course at 8 a.m. There would be three complete sets of London dailies and all the fashion magazines, *Tatler*, *Illustrated London News*, etc., which was quite some load to deliver. One set of London dailies was a hefty pile of papers and as much as I could manage to carry any distance. If Mr Esmond happened to be in the party there would be one set for him and one set for the household and yet another complete set for His Lordship.

These people, I am sure, were reading the news, five hundred miles from London, before the papers had arrived in Bognor Regis. The pilot, who delivered the papers, often asked did anyone want a lift back, but I don't think he had many takers. Viscount Rothermere himself would never dream of air travel, but preferred to have his feet firmly on the ground. But he would sail the seven seas and was in his element. He would often be at sea for several months at a time and was probably the most travelled man of his time.

He employed five chauffeurs and owned one Rolls Royce 50, two Rolls Royce 25s and two Pontiacs, oh, and an old Austin staff car that lived at Stody – servants for the use of. Bob Tanner, His Lordship's head chauffeur, would continually be called upon to pick His Lordship up in any place in Europe, when he happened to be travelling further abroad and would maybe want to take a short cut to the south of

France before returning to this country.

The other chauffeurs received their instructions from the secretaries in London. During his long absence from England, His Lordship would have houseguests sent to his various houses, to be entertained by his staff, and many a grand shooting party was held at Stody or grouse shooting on the moors in the north of Scotland.

It was, I remembcr, 1935 when my wife and I were at the Flat together, and there was to be a Thanksgiving Service to commemorate the 25th anniversary of King George V's accession to the Throne, at St Paul's Cathedral, on Monday the 6th May at 11.30 am, to which Viscount Rothermere was invited. His Majesty had been failing in health for some time and it was, I remember, the following January that the nation was to grieve for a good King. His Majesty had passed away peacefully on 20th January 1936 at 11.55 p.m. at Sandringham, and the state telegram arrived at Stratton House, Piccadilly at 6.15 a.m. the following morning, Tuesday 21st January.

I got into immediate contact with F.J.Clark, the secretary, and he referred me to Mr H.Morison His Lordship's financial secretary, who instructed me to hold it for future collection by himself. In the meantime, Lord Rothermere was hurrying back to London. He had left London on the 20th December bound for Morocco on HMS Dempo. I had heard from 'The Professor' (he had arrived into my story now, but I shall mention him again later). He was His Lordship's masseur and always travelled with him.

In the meantime, there is quite some speculation and excitement as his Royal Highness the Prince of Wales is proclaimed officially His Majesty King Edward VIII. We were aware of Mrs Simpson, who was living at Fort Belvedere, and that the stories, political and otherwise, were being splashed all over the newspapers with Stanley Baldwin as the villain of the piece. Here, surprisingly, Sir Walter Monckton pops back into my story as champion of Edward VIII.

But the object of this story is my life and what happened to me, not what I saw and heard. I have, however, made a note in my diary that on Saturday 25th January I went around to Avenue Road to do a dinner party, whilst my wife had Mr Morison and three ladies to dinner at the Flat. The dinner was sent up by the Malmason, later the Le Coc d'Or Restaurant, which, of course, was on the ground floor of Stratton House, and we could order a full course dinner simply by 'phoning down.

On the following Sunday I had another dinner to do at Avenue Road where His Lordship had invited General Fuller, just recently back from the Abyssinian war, General Groves, Mr Harold McMillan, Mr George Ward Price (*Daily Mail* Foreign Correspondent), Mr Colin Brooks and Mr H.Morison. I mention this party as this was similar to many other dinner parties around this time. This particular party didn't break up until 1.30 am.

This brings us up to the special day – my wife and I have been married for one year – 20th April – and this coincided with Hitler's birthday, and we rather begrudged sharing so happy an anniversary with such an unsavoury character.

On Monday, 6th May also there was a special issue of the *Daily Mail*, a Silver Newspaper in honour of King George V's Silver Jubilee, price one shilling. The front page reading as follows:

> ***"Today all ranks and classes in this country and the peoples of the whole Empire will join in loyal and affectionate congratulations to the King and Queen.***
>
> ***"The twenty-five years of their reign have been among the most momentous in history and through all their dangers, sorrows and vicissitudes, whether in peace or the most agonising of wars, Their Majesties have known how to command their subjects devotion and now the story of those troubled years with their tremendous events, is graphically told by Major General Frederick Maurice, one of our ablest historians and soldiers, in this special Daily Mail Silver Jubilee issue.***
>
> ***"After twenty-five years the Throne stands secure, a rock on which the waves of time and revolution have beaten in vain. The contrast of its position with that which it held a century***

*ago, is extraordinary indeed. Then the Monarchy was unpopular and the general opinion was that it was not destined long to survive, and that republicanism was a preferable form of Government. Today its authority is firmly rooted in the hearts of the people and General Hertzog's declaration that he is done with republicanism, correctly represents the trend of modern thought throughout the Empire, and indeed, the World.*

*"The King is regarded everywhere as one of the greatest World figures of our time, and his wisdom, statesmanship and exalted sense of duty have won the admiration of his contemporaries.*

*"The Daily Mail is maintaining its attachment to Britain's eternal past and all that is in it is beautiful and noble, by producing this special number, a unique souvenir of the reign, recalling in pictures and words its most memorable events and portraying in the broadest outline the social aspects of that stormy and heroic age."*

## Chapter VII

# THE DEATH OF KING GEORGE V

**THE FUNERAL** of King George V lives in my memory as I witnessed the procession with my wife from the roof of Stratton House. The funeral cortege passed down Piccadilly, very solemn but spectacular, the Gun Carriage being drawn by able bodied seamen marching slow time to the Funeral March. The surrounding buildings were crowded with people and every inch of space was taken advantage of. We could also see that every window, which overlooked the procession, was full to capacity.

The day following I heard a very interesting story[5] concerning King Carol of Rumania, one of the crowned heads of Europe, attending His Majesty's funeral. He was staying at Claridge's hotel and had been unwell the evening before, and had had the services of the hotel masseur.

The following morning, still not being fully recovered, he insisted that the masseur accompany him to where the procession would commence, this having been accomplished, it left the masseur with no escape route available, and for King Carol, still a little unsteady, the situation looked rather grim. Eventually someone had a bright idea; a black jacket was produced which the masseur was helped into, to disguise his white smock. A trilby hat was then placed upon his head and one medal conjured up from an unknown source, was placed upon

---

5 As might be suspected, there are several different versions of this story on the internet. However the presence in the procession of the oddly dressed gentleman is recorded in the rare photograph at Fig 9.

his left breast. He then walked in the procession beside King Carol and amongst many dignitaries from foreign lands.

I have in my possession a press photograph of this historical incident. It was never published then or at any other time. Lord Rothermere gave me the picture on 11th February 1936 and it is still kept by me as a souvenir.

We were now getting near to the possibility of war, and it was the constant subject of conversation. In June 1936, Herr Von Ribbentrop lunched at Stratton House. Princess Stephanie Hohenlohe began to be a regular visitor around about the same time. A rather fascinating lady of middle age and most attractively dressed, with the most expensive perfume, which would announce her arrival and delay her departure! I could tell, even after three or four hours after her visit, and on many occasions, having had to absent myself for other duties, on returning to the Flat, there was no need to ask my wife if the Princess had paid a visit. There were often times when His Lordship had no wish to see her, and I was notified by the secretary on these occasions. So when she arrived at Stratton House I would tell her His Lordship was in Norfolk, or the south of France – never mind where – just as long as I could get rid of her.

When on one such a day I had been talking to Her Highness and telling her how far away His Lordship was at that particular time, and had already got the door open prior to her departure, His Lordship stepped into the corridor from his sitting room and boomed "Good morning my dear, won't you come in?" The princess gave me a sidelong look and a purposeful smile as she passed down the corridor to be greeted by Lord Rothermere. At the same time another regular visitor was at the door and on entering, leaned toward me and remarked "Chinnock, next to Jimmy Clark you are the biggest liar I know."

At a later date, I received a telephone call and it was the Princess again, "Hello Chinnock," she began "I'm speaking from the south of France, where is Lord Rothermere please?" Actually, he was at the time spending a short stay in Norfolk, but, of course, I had my instructions and so I told the Princess that Lord Rothermere was in Berlin. "Thank you and goodbye."

However, much to my amazement a few hours afterwards I received another telephone call – this one from Berlin. "Hello Chinnock, this is Princess Hohenlohe and I am in Berlin and Lord Rothermere is not here." She was quite frequently known to travel by air and was very mobile, so on this occasion I apologised and said that was the information I was given, your Highness."

Here is a good time to introduce Mr George Honour; he was His Lordship's masseur. He was discovered on an Atlantic liner. Lord Rothermere found his ministrations effective so gave him the job of looking after him personally. He was of course a trained masseur, and Lord Rothermere and his friends jocularly referred to him as 'The Professor'. He travelled everywhere with him and the staff also referred to George as 'The Professor'. In his coming and goings, especially after a trip to Berchtesgaden when His Lordship would visit Herr Hitler, the German Chancellor, I would joke, and ask "what time is the war to begin then?" and 'The Professor' would reply "Half past two next Wednesday." or some such nonsense. For of course in those early days just before the war there was a lot of speculation, but that was for the politicians of my day to worry about, I was on the sidelines watching current events.

At the same time, I was quite busy doing my own job. Mr Winston Churchill often popped into Stratton House and once, His Lordship having walked out of his sitting room just at the moment I had taken Mr Churchill's gold knobbed walking cane and well-known hat, he walked towards us, placed an arm around Mr Churchill's shoulders and one arm around my own, and as he wheeled us both around to walk down the corridor to his sitting room, he said "Chinnock, if you want to be Mr Winston Churchill's friend for life always meet him at the door with a big cigar and a bottle of whisky."

In manner both these men would seem abrupt to the point of aggressiveness, but underneath would shine out two very human and amiable men.

There was another occasion when I was with Lord Rothermere in his sitting room, tidying up a mountain of newspapers which he had been reading, when he decided to pay a visit to an adjacent bathroom. He had only been absent for about a minute when his telephone rang – his private telephone that is – so I picked up the receiver and a voice said, "Hello, I have Mr Winston Churchill on the line for His Lordship."

"Will you put him on please." I replied, as Lord Rothermere had just appeared at the door.

"Who is on the 'phone Chinnock?" he asked me,

"Mr Winston Churchill" said I.

"Do you imagine I talk to anyone who cares to ring me up?" he asked?

"No, My Lord."

"Then please don't presume in future."

"No, My Lord."

Exit Chinnock; and as I departed, I heard a very hearty "Hello Winston!" from His Lordship.

One day Lord Rothermere was having a conference and there were about six important persons with him in his sitting room. I was summoned by the bell and duly appeared in the room, where I stood awaiting His Lordship's wishes. Much to my amazement, the whole group turned their eyes towards me but not a word was spoken. After about a minute, His Lordship said, "Alright Chinnock you may go now." Feeling very puzzled and wishing to find out what it was all about I went to see F.J.Clark one of the secretaries, whose office was next door to His Lordship's sitting room. On telling him what had happened he laughed and said, "Yes, I know what it was about; Lord Rothermere had said to his company, 'Have you ever noticed Chinnock's legs, he has the most extraordinary long ones.'" To prove his point had sent for me to be inspected by one and all. I do possess very long legs; I was six feet two and a half inches tall, but when dressed in full morning dress and tails my legs would naturally stand out.

When His Lordship was in residence, I would have three complete changes a day, short black jacket and vest and London trousers first thing in the morning. By mid-morning full morning dress with tails and in the evening full evening dress suit with black tie.

Lord Rothermere was a most fastidious man and would insist on the highest order where cleanliness was concerned, not only for himself but also for his whole household. The linen was immaculate and no one used a serviette or tablecloth more than once. Guest towels, likewise, were used once only and His Lordship's bed linen was changed the moment he left his bedroom.

He would rise at 5 o'clock in the morning for his walk. Tanner, the chauffeur, would be waiting at the front door with the Rolls maybe at Norfolk or in Scotland when he would drive His Lordship into the countryside. "Alright Tanner, stop here." and His Lordship would commence his morning walk. Tanner meanwhile would sit in the car and watch him out of sight then follow to the next corner for another vantage point where he could keep him in view. He would be discreet in the performance of his duty and eventually His Lordship would signal that he had had his walk. Whereupon Tanner would pick him up again and bring him home. I would be waiting to receive him, his beloved newspapers were already in his bedroom and 'The Professor' would be somewhere in the vicinity always available, as were all his staff. In the meantime, his bed had been stripped and remade with fresh crisp clean linen sheets. His Lordship invariably went straight to his bedroom where he would change into fresh clean pyjamas and return to his bed to read his newspapers and, in between whiles, decide what he would like for breakfast, which would be taken to him.

The housemaids would have been up since about 4 a.m. doing their various duties. Nearly all the fireplaces were made of steel which were regularly burnished, but they all managed to keep out of His Lordship's way, and he hardly ever saw a servant during the early hours, though there was quite a lot of activity.

The footmen would have laid breakfast in the dining room for the other house-guests, who after breakfasting could expect to see His Lordship re-appear about ten o'clock. When he vacated his room, the head housemaid would again strip his bed even though they had only been used for two to three hours, fresh laundered sheets were put on.

In a country house of such style, there was so much going on all the time, each department was fully occupied, whenever there were residents. Quite often, there were long periods with just the staff, and it was possible to be without any houseguests for as long as three months at a stretch. Consequently, when we were busy, everyone worked to capacity. Cleaning silver in the butler's pantry was a ritual, all the silver being kept in the strong-room which was furnished with green baize. Shelves and overhangs of lead-weighted baize folded back over the silver on the shelves. This was always kept in tip-top condition; added to this were the baize-lined canteens, trunk size, with lift out trays of beautiful table cutlery and silver. Silver was cleaned every day. When we had guests, there was sufficient silver for two complete covers, so that the silver used on one day was, after being washed, placed on a tray and covered by a clean pantry cloth. This would eventually contain the whole day's used silver, which would then be returned to the strong-room. On day two, the footmen would clean all the previous day's silver. This method ensured that no silver, other than clean silver, ever entered the dining room.

Some of the silver was heavily chased, and this would call for special attention. Our footmen's tricks of the trade were to use match sticks with well chewed ends which were then dipped into the Goddard's plate powder and methylated spirit and carefully worked into the crevices. I say carefully, as often it may be George III silver, or that made by Paul Lamerie, and once or twice a month we would use Jewellers' Rouge as well. Most of the work was done with the finger tips, which when impregnated with powder and methylated spirit, became as soft as silk.

I could write at great length on the subject of cleaning silver, including antiques, which of course are valued by weight and accordingly must not be harshly treated. So the secret of cleaning silver then is to have the proper tools for the job, the right kind and size of plate brushes, the finest leathers, but most important of all, these must be kept scrupulously clean. Even with all these aids, believe me, cleaning silver is jolly hard work, but it helps if one loves beautiful things.

Whilst still at Stratton House, Lord Rothermere had presented my wife with a beautiful Maltese terrier puppy with which she was delighted. So we quickly read up notes regarding its diet. We also got

Johnson's baby powder and an electric hair dryer, a steel comb and a brush. She was absolutely beautiful but she needed much attention. We soon had her looking very 'with it', however, with a pink bow on her head. She was very much admired, and often when walking along Piccadilly, my wife would carry her in her arms and she would be the centre of attraction, especially if it was early evening when the ladies and gentlemen were entering or leaving the hotels and restaurants. We would take her daily into the Green Park where, after a ten minute run around, she would return with very black feet.

One Sunday morning I took Judy (for this was her name – and she had a brother Punch, who lived at Avenue Road, Swiss Collage) a little further afield. We chose to go for a walk in Hyde Park, and walked up the avenue of trees adjacent to Rotten Row. It was a lovely spring morning, with not many people about, but as we progressed towards Kensington Gardens, Judy ran in front of me towards two people, a lady and a gentleman, and as she drew near, she commenced to bark alarmingly. I dashed forward to pick her up and having secured her, I turned to address the lady and gentleman, when to my utter surprise I realised I was in the presence of the Duke and Duchess of Kent. "Good morning" she was saying.

"Good morning your Highness." I said, then they were both talking about the delightful little dog, and after standing talking to the Royal pair for at least ten minutes, they said their good mornings again and took their leave of me.

I was happy with my experience and went back to the Flat to tell my wife very casually, who I had been talking to in the park. Princess Marina was one of our favourite Royals; the other was the Duchess of Gloucester. My wife took a great interest in society as a whole and I remember she took herself off one day to go to the wedding of the Duke of Norfolk, at the Brompton Oratory. Incidentally, we were both present at the Duke of Norfolk's funeral, only a year or so past,[6] at Arundel Cathedral, but I must go back in time again.

---

6 The funeral took place on 6th April 1975

The Flat in Stratton House was the place where we came into contact with many celebrities. Mr Walter Hackett, the playwright and his wife, Marion Lorne lived in the Flat immediately below us, and a couple of floors lower we had another quite famous actress, Madeleine Carroll, and across the other side of the road was the Ritz Hotel, where we often saw the Aga Khan, who spent quite a lot of time there. We also often saw his son Ali who was another of the set that The Hon Esmond Harmsworth, who lived in Warwick House, St James's, mixed with, also H.R.H. The Prince of Wales.

## Chapter VIII

# ESMOND HARMSWORTH

**THE HON ESMOND HARMSWORTH** was a most remarkable man, being the only surviving son, his two older brothers both having been killed in the 1914-1918 war. Had they been spared, one could only try to imagine what magnificent futures they would have enjoyed. To return to Mr Esmond, he was a most charming man, whose instant smile would melt anyone's heart. He was six feet four inches tall, and as I was only six feet two inches I had to look up to him. He had a charming family, Miss Lorna, Miss Esmie, and Master Vere, all blessed with the family's good looks and, indeed I say, money.

From time to time they all visited Lord Rothermere at Stratton House, and Master Vere came in for a strawberry and cream tea quite frequently. So much was going on, however, with the abdication of H.M. King Edward VIII and the looming clouds of war, which at that time was the popular topic of conversation, but in between times we indulged in happiness, hoping that the world would somehow regain its sanity.

After eating some heather honey with his tea one day, His Lordship said "Chinnock, I'm wondering how many different kinds of honey there are. Get on to Fortnum & Mason's and ask them to send me as many different kinds of honey as they can lay hands on."

The outcome of that little experiment was quite hair-raising. I had never in my life seen such an assortment of exotic jars and containers as they sent for our inspection, from all parts of the world. I had hoped to record the different species but unfortunately, I never got around to actually doing so. Things happened so quickly in those days. A lot of the honey was sent to Avenue Road, and His Lordship gave quite a lot away to his friends.

Mr Esmond arrived at the Flat one day, "Hello, Benny Boy" said His Lordship, that being his pet name. It's your birthday, what can I give you for a present?"

"Oh, nothing thank you," said Mr Esmond.

"Let me put £10,000 in your account."

"No, really, father, I have plenty of money."

"Well now, isn't it about time you engaged a valet? You are the richest young man in London and you haven't got one. It's really time that you replaced Sutton."

Sutton had been Mr Esmond's valet, but had been dismissed his service the previous year, for reasons best not mentioned. At that time, Mr Esmond was certainly not thinking of doing so. It was always so nice to see him, with his father, he was so vital and charming and his smile was so infectious. I know His Lordship delighted in his company, all 6ft.4ins of him, dressed in the best Saville Row style and certainly one of the best-dressed men in town. Another I might mention was Mr Anthony Eden, the Foreign Secretary, whom I also met on several occasions.

Mr Esmond, as we always called him, was a frequent visitor to Stody Lodge at this time and one of his motor cars was a beautiful Rolls- Bentley which he would often drive himself whilst his chauffeur sat beside him.

At this time also, Sir Oswald Moseley was often interviewed. His Black Shirts Movement was taking up a great deal of news space. What with the National League of Airmen on the one hand, the Black Shirts, and Hitler's Brown Shirts, and Marshal Goering's Air Force on the other; the daily news was quite foreboding. It was a kind of light relief, in a way, to have Edward VIII and Mrs Simpson to take peoples' minds off the inevitable war that loomed ahead.

Everyone, suddenly, became aware of Fort Belvedere. We had often, in the past, heard the Prince of Wales as he motored through the West End, for his was the first musical motor horn that, I think, was permitted to be used, and now he had become a King.

The Duke and Duchess of York then lived at the Knightsbridge end of Piccadilly, 145 Piccadilly, if my memory serves me right, and to be sure my wife and I on many occasions had seen the Royal children at play in their garden, and with their Nanny, Crawfie, and history was developing at a most incredible rate.

King George VI with his Queen had their Coronation in 1937, and the cheers of the London crowd did something to efface their hidden thoughts of the terrible war that was to erupt within the next two years, and so the nation celebrated as only an English crowd knows how. The press was full of happy pictures of the Royal couple and their children, Princess Elizabeth and her younger sister, Princess Margaret.

Princess Elizabeth had a special remembrance for me as she had been born in Bruton Street and so touches upon my birthplace.

But those were very grim times indeed and it would be the task of our new King to pilot us through the war that would soon be upon us.

## Chapter IX

# LIFE AT BURGHFIELD HOUSE

**NOW IS THE TIME** when my own family takes up the limelight, as my wife is expecting our first child – nothing unusual about that, you may think. We were in London at the time and when His Lordship came in one morning, he said to my wife "Rose my dear, I want you to go to Burghfield (Burghfield House, Dornoch, Sutherland, Scotland), Chinnock can stay behind as I want him in London."

And so it was, I in London and my wife in Scotland and she would be about three months pregnant but had not as yet seen a doctor to confirm or deny. Some of the staff knew of the situation and some of the ladies had heard rumours and often I was asked by one or the other of them, "Is it true Chinnock that Rose is going to have a baby?" I could only say, "I think so."

Most days I would get a telephone call from Dornoch to keep me informed, my wife each time asking me "When are you coming to Scotland?"

"When the Old Man tells me." I'd say.

To the servants 'The Old Man' was a title of respect – Churchill and Beaverbrook also bore this title so we would always add '*Our* Old Man' to make sure of being perfectly understood. His Lordship, at this time, being in Scotland and having no doubt heard these whispers from the ladies that Chinnock's wife was expecting a baby said, "Well, why isn't he here with her?" and forthwith I was notified to be on the evening train for Inverness. No second bidding required; I was so happy to be on my way to see my wife once again.

When I eventually arrived at the House, and at the earliest opportunity, His Lordship sent for me, he said, "What's this I hear about Rose having a baby?"

I replied, "Well, I think so My Lord."

"So it's not confirmed, well get Dr Neal to examine her. He will soon tell us all if it's true."

Dr Neal was a house-guest and a very charming old gentleman who enjoyed fishing on the Loch and who was transported there by pony whenever he wished to go. I had been with him myself once or twice, so when I said, "Dr Neal, My Lord?" thinking maybe my wife may be a little embarrassed. Maybe it wasn't what I said but how I said it that evoked His Lordship to say "What's the matter Chinnock, isn't Dr Neal good enough? He brought my children into the world you know, so when you know something definite come and tell me please."

You may be sure I went straight away to Dr Neal and explained the situation. "I understand," he said, "and don't think any more about it. Just take me to your wife and we will soon have the situation sorted out."

I don't know what we expected, but when he came into our bedroom, he said, "Hello my dear, if you will just lay down on your back and don't be embarrassed – I only want to feel your tummy."

He did precisely that and after a short while said, "Yes, Chinnock, your wife is pregnant so you can now take your message to His Lordship." I did so of course and received his congratulations. Soon all the houseguests were talking about the happy event to come and I was proud to be me; but soon we were back into the routine once again.

We had quite a large house party that summer. Lord Rothermere was a very simple and understanding person, and I knew that just as long as there were no mistakes and the house ran on oiled wheels, there would be no cause to be 'called on the mat'. I said 'simple' just now, so I must explain myself – if he ever said, "Chinnock bring me a cup of tea" he meant just that – a cup of tea on a silver salver, and he was always to the point.

Talking about tea reminds me that whenever we were in Dornoch we always made sure we had ample supplies of Evian water. The reason for this was that the water supply locally was very discoloured owing to the peat content, so we transported cases of Evian water from London for tea making and cooking purposes. Incidentally, peat water was absolutely super for the bath and was very soft. I remember the first time I ran a bath of water at Burghfield House I thought all the pipes must be rusty, but was assured by the housekeeper that it was usual and she explained the reason.

Having the telephone direct to the *Daily Mail*, it was a simple task to get supplies put on a passenger train, whether it be Imperial oysters from Scott's of Piccadilly or choice pears from Fortnum and Mason's.

I remember that summer walking out on the lawn where the footmen were serving tea to the ladies, when His Lordship arose from his chair and came walking towards me with a bemused look and a glance upwards, said, "Chinnock, what kind of bird is that do you suppose?"

"Oh, that's a plover My Lord."

"Oh, is it?" he said and passed on.

Sometime later the same situation arose only this time His Lordship had a positive grin on his face as he approached and said, "Chinnock, what kind of bird is that then?" and looked up.

I replied, "That is a great black-backed gull." That stopped him in his tracks.

"Chinnock, do you know what you are talking about?"

"Yes My Lord, I am very interested in birds."

"I hope you stick to the feathered variety!" He laughed as he went on his way.

He was absolutely in touch; sometimes he would say to me, "Chinnock, read me some of those book titles." I would read several and he would say, "That's all, thanks Chinnock."

Another time he had had his complete set of London daily newspapers and had sat in his great easy chair with his feet upon a pouf avidly reading and discarding papers read in a huge pile on the floor. I entered the sitting room and discovered him to be fast asleep, so I took the opportunity to gather up and fold the discarded newspapers and replace them in a neat pile. All this done without arousing His Lordship. I was about to leave the room when I noticed he had the *Times* spread across his knees, so very carefully, so as not to waken him, I started to remove the paper when quite suddenly and in a gruff voice he said, "You can leave that one, Chinnock, it's keeping my knees warm!"

That summer in Scotland was a memorable one for me. We had had lovely weather and His Lordship was in fine fettle. He had a grand sense of humour and would often say to one or other of the gentlemen guests, "Have you played golf on the Dornoch course, it's very good I believe." And after leading them on for a little while would say, "Golf – well I bet my head gardener could beat you at the game, in fact I'll bet you a fiver." And, having said that, would chuckle to himself because he knew and I knew that his gardener, Wattie Ross, was a plus three man.

It was rarely that His Lordship was without a following. George Ward Price, Foreign Correspondent of the *Daily Mail*, Mr Colin Brookes and a couple of secretaries were almost always there when important events were afoot, and he spent many months travelling the world. One thing I thought was most unusual about him, he very rarely wore jewellery of any kind, not even a pocket watch or wristwatch, but with such a following he need only ask the time. I'm sure he lived every minute of it, and one of his utterances always stays in my mind, "But I say, what a world?"

After a few weeks at Dornoch, His Lordship decides he is going back to London. So he sends for me and says, "We are going back to London tomorrow Chinnock, that is I am, and the houseguests, but you are to stay here for another two weeks with your wife. I want you to take great care of her, tell her she can have whatever she wants. She can take all my books out on the lawn if she likes, the staff can look after you, and I will leave you a car and a chauffeur to take you anywhere you wish to go."

This VIP treatment was so typical of the man, he was so generous and kind and I was always at liberty to help myself from a very large cellar to any wine. This privilege I never ever abused, and I have always been a very temperate man.

We spent a very happy time in Dornoch. We had of course Judy, our little Maltese terrier with us, and she went everywhere with us, needless to say. There was a small resident staff at Burghfield House and we were feeling like Royalty.

The chauffeur would come to our bidding and we had many lovely trips. We would go to the Hotel at John O'Groats for luncheon sometimes, or go over to the west coast to Ullapool, our happiness only being marred by the fact that we often had to stop, owing to my wife feeling sick, but tour the Highlands we did and enjoyed the most lovely weather.

Scotland is a very beautiful place, and about that time, the Lochness Monster was very much in the news. We went many times to see if we could catch a glimpse of the fabulous creature. Pictures had been taken, postcards depicting this creature were on sale, the monks at Fort Augustus, when interviewed by pressmen, agreed that there was some strange beastie in the loch, but I'm afraid I always took it with a pinch of salt, a good tourist gimmick maybe, but the story seems to persist even until today.

True it was that people had not all had the same opportunity to visit and appreciate the beauties of the Highlands, but the motor car was gradually coming into its own and more people ventured to the unspoiled loveliness of Scotland. And the older I get the more I am convinced that there isn't a finer sight in the rest of the world than the remote Highlands in all their beauty. I am speaking as a naturalist perhaps – but certainly, it takes a lot of beating.

Of course, we were privileged people and everywhere we went, we were treated with the utmost kindness – everyone had time for us, everyone was interested. In fact it was a different world to live in; in those days there was always time to stand and stare and I'll always remember the serenity of the crofter's cottage and the wholesome food and girdle cakes and the simple folk who were nothing if not genuine.

We were invited to tea on one occasion so with Judy, our little dog, my wife and I made our way across the open heather-clad hillside towards a crofter's cottage where lived the family of a young lady whom we had met on the train and who had a situation in London with the Fearnley-Whittingstalls. Suddenly Judy decided that chasing sheep was fair game, so off she bounded and soon had a fair sized flock. Fortunately she was only a toy dog and I was able to catch her and order was restored, but the little dog was still very interested in the chase, so we had to carry her the rest of the way, and so we arrived and were invited into the crofter's cottage that was so neat and clean with a beautiful tea spread on a plain table. We were entertained, made to feel at home, and spent a most enjoyable time with the family. We kept in touch with the young lady and at a later date, we met her again in London.

The West Coast of Scotland we liked very much and enjoyed the salmon jumping in the River Shinn. His Lordship had a grouse moor and the keeper or gillie kept the game dogs in five kennels. I often watched them fed and sometimes I would accompany him on training programmes when the dogs were worked to retrieve and the pointers to point game. Mostly they worked to a whistle and it was an education to see them put through their paces. They were beautiful animals, but essentially working dogs, so were never petted – or should I say very rarely – because there was one black retriever I remember always seemed to cash-in when we stopped for picnic lunch during a shoot and who would nuzzle up to anyone present to ask for a tit-bit. I think he must have been the granddad of the bunch; in any case, he was the only one with such a privilege.

# Chapter X

# FISHING WITH DR NEAL

I RECALL FISHING in the loch with Dr Neal. The gillie would bring the pony and having got the old gentleman into the saddle we would, with the fishing equipment and packed luncheon, proceed across the moor and upwards towards the loch, where the gillie would get the boat out of the small boathouse and would stow us with our fishing equipment into the boat where we were left to our own devices.

As I said before Dr Neal was an elderly and interesting gentleman and took great pleasure in instructing me in the art of fly-fishing. The assortment of fishing flies in his hat was a picture to behold. I can't remember the names of the various flies but according to the doctor they all had one and he could cast in the most amazing fashion and drop his fly practically where he liked. So I decided that I would fish from the opposite side of the boat so as not to interfere with his expert casting. Nevertheless, I had considerable success and much enjoyed his friendly encouragement.

In so silent a place, just two people in a boat, at peace with the world, and not another soul to be seen – even the gillie would be about a mile away awaiting our return – and so with content we would fish and when having caught a trout it seemed to cause such a commotion as would shatter our solitude.

When Dr Neal decided he would like to eat, we would row back to where we would find the gillie waiting with his two dogs near the boathouse. I would unpack the lunch basket for us to do justice to our appetites, the open air and exercise having put a suitable edge on mine, anyway, and I suspected on the others likewise. However, the picnic lunch was quite adequate and the couple of bottles of hock and a few pints of beer were more than sufficient for our needs.

Over lunch the subjects for conversation were varied, the quality of the catch, or the grouse moors, and the gillie would fill us in with all the local gossip. One story he told was of illicit stills in the Highlands. I was interested in this fact because at an earlier date I had been offered a drink of whisky that had been made locally, it was perfectly clear though it smelt unmistakably whisky-like. I accepted and drank the sample and can assure you it was a very potent brew. The gillie talked also of a great black-backed gull that was taking trout from the loch, and he suggested there was a nest on a small island at the centre of the loch with hungry young ones waiting to be fed. He would, he said, attend to that at an early date.

After lunch, we would fish again for a couple of hours before we would begin our journey back across the heather homeward bound. We went always pretty well loaded as, never knowing what the weather would do, we had to take suitable precautions and, of course, often took clothing that we never used. When the weather is settled it can be so nice, but in changeable conditions, we had to be prepared for any kind of situation. However, I used to try to arrange to get Dr Neal back to the house by about 5 o'clock as that would give him ample time to take a bath and have a little light refreshment before dinner which was usually about 8 o'clock.

I must, I think, now get back to the moment in time where my wife and I are left on our own at Dornoch. We both had a most enjoyable stay, and the experience was one of a lifetime. Who can say what it feels like to be living in a grand house in the Highlands unless they have had it happen to them? My wife and I, for our part, were in a veritable fairyland and were very happy.

Mr John Sutherland, the town clerk and our great friend, asked us if we would care to accompany him to an estate in Ross & Cromarty which he managed for some wealthy clients. We decided that we would like to take advantage of his kind offer and off we went. It was a glorious drive through the countryside and, having arrived at the estate office, we were introduced to the Land Agent and his staff who took a great delight in showing us around the antler bedecked wooden buildings adjoining the estate office and outbuildings, as John Sutherland had left us in order to attend to the business which had brought us hither.

The agent took us on a walk around, the honeysuckle was most abundant and the perfume was heady, it was at its prime and I happened to say how beautiful it was and referred to it as wild woodbine at which the agent agreed and said, "That's not common knowledge; most people only ever refer to honeysuckle as such." I expressed a wish to take a root away with me upon which he remarked that the time was not right to attempt transplants, but he was eager to accommodate me and said, "If you will leave an address to which I may send you a couple of roots at the appropriate time, I would be pleased to do so." I thanked him very much and left my home address in Somersetshire, as at that time I had no personal address. My wife and I were travelling around to various houses of Lord Rothermere and having our headquarters at the Flat in Stratton House in London.

John Sutherland had returned shortly and after thanking our temporary hosts for their kindness, we took our leave and returned to Dornoch having had a very enjoyable day's outing. A few months later, I was to get a letter from my mother in Somerset asking if I could solve the mystery of a parcel of honeysuckle saplings received from somewhere in Scotland. I had forgotten to mention the arrangement, and I was pleasantly surprised and explained the situation to her. I do know that the honeysuckle was planted and did very well and, as far as I know, is still spreading its annual perfume around the Somersetshire village of Bruton.

The time arrived when it was necessary for us to say goodbye to Burghfield House once more and return to London, so after the round of farewells, we were driven to Bonar Bridge and entrained to London via Inverness. We enjoyed our time on the train, it was always a very good service, and the food was highly commendable.

We eventually arrived at the Flat in Stratton House at our leisure, as His Lordship was still away in the south of France. It goes without saying of course that Judy, our little Maltese terrier, was our constant companion and was a very good ambassador at all times and very apt at introducing herself and us.

I ran an expense account and, when it so happened I was running short of cash, I could be reimbursed by the secretary just for the asking, and whilst living at the Flat in Stratton House in His Lordship's absence, we lived on a Board Wages Agreement which was paid weekly by the secretary. We would often have spells of a couple of months when His Lordship was abroad, with one or other of the secretaries popping in to attend to the incoming mail.

My wife had received a letter from His Lordship dated 10th July 1937 stating the following:

*Sanatorium Dr F Dengler*
*Baden-Baden*
*July 10*

*Dear Rose,*

*When a girl is engaged she wears a pretty ring on her finger, but how does a dog announce such news to the world? I suppose by a pink bow round her neck fastened with love knots.*

*You must buy a pretty silk one because His Lordship asks me to convey to you the news that your little dog is engaged, and so must conduct herself with the dignity and aloofness that are becoming to a fiancé. If brazen Aberdeens or skittish Skyes try to give her what I believe is commonly known as the 'glad eye', she must pass them by with nose in the air and not even bat an eyelid to admit that she is aware of their existence.*

*I hope you are having a good time at Dornoch.*

*Yours very faithfully*

*H. Morison.*

We were told His Lordship was on his way home, we had a date too, so the Flat was got in readiness and, with much ado, we busied ourselves and at the appointed time the flowers were ordered.

Gerrard's of Bond Street sent some especially nice bowls of very tastefully arranged blooms so that His Lordship's sitting room was a sight to behold, not to mention a grand Van Eyck panel portrait of a Man 8½ x 11 inches, value at that time £25,000.

His Lordship's collection of pictures at that time ran into millions of pounds – Guardis, Canalettos, Tinorettos, Botticellis, El Grecos, Vermeer (The Parable of the Unfaithful Servant) 31½ x 23 inches (£20,000 1938 price) to name but a few. His collection was catalogued and I was familiar with quite a few as, of course, if people were being shown around one of his houses and I happened to be present, it would fall to my lot to explain certain pictures or, maybe, Canton enamel. So it was to my advantage to read up and to be familiar so as to be able to say something to visitors wishing to know. Pictures can, of course, be very technical indeed, so it was nice to have a reference to go to. I am afraid I would be completely out of touch with present day prices – £100,000,000 could be comparable perhaps (for such a collection of masterpieces).

Let's go back to Stratton House where there were a set of George III Tapestry Chairs at £1,000 each (1938 price tag) in the hallway.

On one occasion I had been dispatched to Dornoch, leaving my wife behind in London so for company, she had invited two friends of ours Dai and Novello to stay at the Flat with her for one week. They lived in Kensington. David worked for Elizabeth Arden and Novello worked in Harrods of Knightsbridge. We had been friends for many years, so one can imagine they looked forward to a week of high living in many ways. So at the appointed time they arrived at the Flat and before unpacking, were about to indulge in cold ham and fresh salad with fruit salad and cream for afters, when I chose to ring from Scotland. "Hello Darling," I said, "His Lordship wants you to join me at Burghfield House, come as soon as possible and that means tonight!" So, readers, you will see that our friends never ever got the week they nearly spent with my wife at the Flat – that turned out to be a couple of hours. Fortunately, they had not unpacked their belongings and my wife was able to catch the night train to Inverness. The indignity of the story is that her guests had to help her with the washing up so as to enable her to get away in time to catch her train, and they had never forgotten the week they nearly stayed in a millionaire's flat in London.

But back to personalities. His Lordship had arrived; the weather was beautiful. We called it 'Lordie's weather', as he always seemed to follow the sun – or should I say the sun seemed to follow him. So back to the interviewing. In the last few months of 1937, we were meeting people of fame and renown: cabinet ministers, foreign visitors, air marshals and generals. Mr Lloyd George was one such caller and Lord Beaverbrook and, of course, Winston Churchill was quite a regular caller. I was often dispatched to his office in Morpeth Mansions with documents. His Lordship would say, "Chinnock, pop this round to Mr Winston Churchill." So I would jump into a taxi to Morpeth Mansions and on arrival would be ushered straight into the great man's presence. I wasn't to dream as yet that he was to be a very famous Prime Minister of England. I think I did about three of what I now choose to call my 'special duly runs' and can only say my opinion of him was that he was a very kind and 'down to earth' man, and I can understand that a man of his kind would and could enjoy building a pigsty or a wall, or enjoy his other great hobby – painting. I met his son Randolph on several occasions whilst with Lord Rothermere.

## Chapter XI

# THE PRINCESS HOHENLOHE

**PRINCESS STEPHANIE HOHENLOHE** was a frequent caller at the flat about this period. Sometimes His Lordship would and sometimes he would *not* see her. One day having answered the door, Her Highness, and her very expensive mink coat, were revealed.

"Hello Chinnock. Is Lord R in?"

"I'm afraid His Lordship has gone to Norfolk for a few days your Highness."

"When will he return?"

"We are expecting him on Wednesday."

This, of course, was all made up on the spur of the moment.

"Never mind Chinnock, I will call again, by the way how is Rose?"

"She has a headache this afternoon your Highness."

"Oh, I'm so sorry."

I escorted her to the lift and she is whisked away. I went back into the Flat and told my wife Princess Hohenlohe was asking after her health. Twenty minutes later the telephone rang and when I answered it, it was the Princess calling. "Hello Chinnock, can you get a taxi and come to the Dorchester Hotel, Park Lane? I have something for you." When I arrived at the Dorchester Hotel, I was shown up to her suite where she greeted me with "Please be seated." She left me for half a minute and returned with a sealed envelope. "Chinnock," she said, "I am concerned about your wife, in this envelope are some pills, if she takes them her headache will be better, and this is for you to pay the taxi fare." She gave me a more than generous sum of money and I thanked her and took my leave. I thought what a privileged person I was, and wondered whether my wife would even take the pills she had so kindly given us. In those pre-war years, I had, in my own estimation, the No. 1 job of any butler or steward in London, and I was held in very high esteem by Viscount Rothermere, so that I would leave no stone unturned to please him. So many presents and gratuities came my way, so much consideration and kindness. Cartier, the jewellers of Bond Street, representative, Mr Bellenger, often called at the Flat. He was a charming man but sadly was the gentleman who was badly injured in the Mayfair Playboys Case (Lonsdale & Co.) at a Knightsbridge hotel, when he was attacked and robbed of jewellery of some very great value. He often sent us complimentary tickets for West End shows and I quote:

*175 New Bond Street,*
*London, W.1.*
*26th April 1937.*

*W.J.Chinnock, Esq,* (sic)
*c/o The Viscount Rothermere,*
*Stratton House,*
*Piccadilly,*
*W.1.*

*Dear Mr Chinnock,*

*Am enclosing a card for presentation at the Box Office on Tuesday Evening for the Duke of York's Theatre, and do hope that you enjoy the show.*

*Yours truly*
*E.Bellinger.*

Something just great was always happening. History was being made. Dame Laura Knight was interviewed on one occasion I recall and after her departure; His Lordship presented me with four of her canvasses which were tied in a roll. "Here Chinnock," he said, "look after these for me."

I took them away and my wife and I examined them, they were very nice, we thought. All of them were scenes from the circus with dappled horses. I remember, for the want of a better place, I rolled them all up again and put them under a bed in the spare room, and that, for me, was the last I ever saw of them because in a few months time I was sent away from Stratton House forever, and in the ensuing events, instances like the above would be forgotten. I have often wondered, since, what happened to those four pictures (wherever they are now they must be a very valuable possession to someone).

There was also a painting of His Lordship in his Coronation Robes, by Philip de László, which stood inside the hall cloaks cupboard awaiting a more permanent and dignified site. This was apt to be quite startling, as upon opening the door the picture was floodlit by the concealed light switch being released to reveal the very life-like face of Lord Rothermere.

The names of the personalities calling for the next few months were too many to recall – Sir Robert Vansittart, and, of course, I could go on name-dropping, but be sure that anyone who was anyone at that time in history eventually walked through Viscount Rothermere's doorway.

By this time early 1938, my wife was getting near the end of her pregnancy and His Lordship was constantly asking, "How is your wife, Chinnock?" I kept him informed, and one day he said, "Look here Chinnock, when the time is ripe, Rose can go into the finest nursing home in London, but be advised by Dr Neal, get in touch with him."

Upon so doing and on putting him into the picture, Dr Neal smiled and said, "The finest nursing home in London, well, that's a debatable point, but if you want your wife delivered of her baby at the finest place in London, then that is the Middlesex Hospital, and as the Matron there is a very good friend of mine, I suggest you leave your wife in her capable hands. I will get in touch and arrange for her to be taken in at the appropriate time."

All of this came to pass with the usual anxiety that any first time father is well aware of. I was happy the day I collected my wife and her precious bundle! A little girl weighing 10lb 6½oz who was christened

Hilary Marguerite Ann, and together we returned to Stratton House. The date of birth was 11th March 1938.

There was such excitement showing our newborn off. His Lordship, who was in the South of France, sent the following cablegram:

> ***Dear Rose***
>
> ***So glad to hear you have become a Mother, when so many women are shirking maternity.***
>
> ***Rothermere***

We were so pleased that we had received such a communication from such an illustrious person. Needless to say, we still have that cablegram among our souvenirs.

# Chapter XII

# MY TRIP TO NEW YORK WITH VERE

**ABOUT THE END OF MARCH**, His Lordship returned to London and on our next meeting greeted me with his congratulations. I thanked him and he looked me in the eye and said, "I suppose you think it's the only baby in the world."

"Yes!" I was quick to rejoin.

"That's where you make a mistake my lad, my first baby was! However, you look rather wan; I think a change of air might do you good."

"Do you think so My Lord?" I replied.

"Yes" he said, "How would you like to come to New York with me?"

"Oh, thank you My Lord, I would like that very much."

"Alright laddie, off you go around to the American Consulate and get your visa fixed up. We will be leaving next Wednesday."

Speechless, I took my leave to tell my wife the news. After all, it was she that had had a baby and I was collecting such a bonus and having to leave her at such short notice, but that's how things happened I'm afraid. He was such a spontaneous person. It was uncanny in the fact that this day, 31st March, happened to be my own birthday.

So now, having got all my necessary papers – incidentally my visa from the American Embassy was stamped *GRATIS*, which I thought very special – I discovered I was to be aboard the luxury German ship the *SS Europa* on the 6th April 1938, in a first class cabin.

As yet, I was unaware of any duties I may be called upon to perform, but at that moment I was to be a guest as far as I could understand. 'The Professor', of course, would be travelling with His Lordship as usual.

On joining the ship, however, I discovered that the passenger list included, The Hon Esmond C.Harmsworth, his daughter, The Hon Lorna P.V.Harmsworth and The Hon Vere Harold E.Harmsworth. Miss Lorna was a delightful young woman and at seventeen years old already had her personal maid, a young lady named Gladys M.Mousley.

The *SS Europa* was a fantastic ship, which, at that time had a sister ship the *SS Bremen.* These two were known to be the fastest German ships on the Southampton – Cherbourg – New York run. The *Europa* certainly impressed me, for, after boarding, I lost no time in looking her over after, of course, having stowed our baggage etc., and meeting up with The Hon Esmond and Vere. Miss Lorna and her maid, no doubt, were busy doing their own thing somewhere aboard and getting their luggage stowed. So, after the preliminaries, Mr Esmond, having spoken to me and asked after my health, had left me looking after his charming twelve year old son on holiday from Eaton. He knew me, of course, from his strawberry and cream tea parties that I have mentioned before.

I decided there and then that I would attach myself to Master Vere, whilst aboard ship, and keep him out of mischief if that was going to be tactfully necessary. I met up with 'The Professor' and found the location of all our party's cabins and before we knew it, we had left Southampton and were making way down Southampton Water.

I began once again to explore the ship, but this time I had a young companion to accompany me, and we both enjoyed the experience. On so vast a ship, twice around the deck was approximately one mile, and the public rooms and bars were just grand. There was no need to try to do too much, as we would be aboard for the next five days and there was so much to interest a young man's fancy. We had, it seemed, just become accustomed to the ship's movement when we were already pulling into Cherbourg to pick up more passengers for New York. We were able to watch passengers saying their tearful farewells. Meanwhile a brass band played on the jetty and after a short while we once again put to sea, only this time it would be 3,000 miles before we would land.

As we left Cherbourg, streamers were being thrown overboard to people waving below and the French brass band struck up that tear-jerker *Come back, oh come back, oh come back my bonnie to me, (sic)* and my heart popped back to my wife and baby in England, and a tear welled up in my eye, then I controlled myself. I must, of course, in Master Vere's company, or he would be asking me what it's all about.

So I watched the people recede into the background. The band got less and less coherent *(sic)* and we were all at sea once more. I felt very secure in that great ship – almost 50,000 tonnage she was, and in May 1930 had crossed the Atlantic in 4 days 17 hours and 6 minutes, thus making a record.

Master Vere was twelve years of age at this time, a very good-looking young man with a very engaging personality. He was full of fun and eager to be starting this adventurous trip and I was quite at a loss at times to answer his very forthright questions, for of course, I must find out about this great ship myself. So we explored together and asked questions of the German crew, of whom, incidentally, quite a number could speak very good English. We were both at a loss to understand why we had such little German currency to spend, and even after reading the following important notice, we were neither of us much wiser, but put it down to the political situation at the time and the popular belief that Second World War was imminent in the not too distant future.

***According to the German regulations governing the control of foreign currency, German coins can be accepted from passengers in payment on board only during the ship's voyage from Europe to New York, and then only within the limits of the RM10 – allowed under these regulations. No German money whatever – be it notes or silver, will be accepted on the homeward voyage from New York to Europe. German coins under RM1, RM2 and RM5, will have to be exchanged for board money with the Purser or paid to him to cover any account for expenses on board. All shops, stalls, and members of the Ship's personnel are strictly forbidden to accept German coins to the value of RM1, RM2***

***and RM5. They are also strictly forbidden to accept Reichsmark notes. We would ask our passengers kindly to strictly observe these regulations.***

But, on this particular day in April 1938 it was a lovely day and we were pleasure bent and so the war could wait.

We continued to explore the ship and discovered a shooting range and it was not long before we were indulging and enjoying ourselves. There was a magnificent swimming pool and deck quoits and many other things to amuse us. There was also a chart which interested us, as it measured the sea miles and kept us informed of the daily performance. So our first day at sea was spent in a general reconnoitre.

After dinner it was soon time to return to our cabins to prepare for sleep, and I was wondering how Master Vere would be feeling. Having tucked him up for the night and taken myself off to my own cabin, I popped back to Master Vere's at intervals until I was sure he was sleeping, and so the first night at sea passed.

The Hon Esmond Harmsworth was travelling without a valet on this trip as he had dismissed his man, Sutton, some months before, so I stepped into the breech and attended to his needs. This arrangement worked very well as I could then keep him in touch with Master Vere's welfare, and the following day, meeting His Lordship by chance on deck, he asked, "Well, how are you, and what are you getting up to?"

"I'm looking after The Hon Esmond My Lord, and keeping an eye on Master Vere."

"That's the stuff my boy," he said as he continued on his walk around the deck, "you do that."

'The Professor', Miss Mousley and myself took our meals together each day from a menu that had to be seen to be believed, it was so large and contained just about the ultimate in food to tempt anyone's palate, from oysters to pâté de foie gras. After meals, we would go our separate ways. I would rejoin Master Vere to start again our daily round, and look for interesting things to do.

About midday, we were surprised by a General Alert, when the ship's crew must report to the boat deck. This was to be a daily exercise, when the assembled crew were stood to attention as on parade, after which the shout went up "Sieg Heil! Sieg Heil! Heil Hitler!" then they would give the Nazi salute then they would dismiss to their various duties. These activities came as a great surprise to me so at the next encounter with our German steward I asked what it was all about and did he agree with the daily performance and was Mr Hitler so popular as he would seem to be? He told me quite frankly his opinion of Adolf was not worth much. I spoke to several of the stewards and most agreed it was all against the grain to have to be bothered with such a parade, but it wasn't prudent to say much about it. The parade was compulsory so must be endured. I often took a drink with some of these stewards and they were very nice people and talked quite frankly about the political situation. So I asked, "When will the war start?"

"Your guess is as good as ours – it could be a year or maybe two, but our hearts are certainly not in it."

So, each day we would try not to be too concerned whilst the performance lasted, and looked forward to our future holiday in New York.

On the following day, we had other things to contend with as we sailed into very heavy seas and the great ship pitched and rolled, when even going down the companionway was quite a difficult operation. From the closed portholes, one could see a raging Atlantic ocean on the portside, whilst on the starboard, the sky looked down and within minutes, the position was reversed, so that we (a heaving mass of 49,746 tons) bobbed wildly from side to side as easily as a cork.

I was getting a bit concerned and constantly asked Master Vere if he was feeling ill. I must confess I felt very green and as Vere looked like I felt, I decided the best place to be was in his cabin where he could lie down and ride the storm. However, he turned out to be an excellent sailor, and though at times we both looked wretched, we were neither of us seasick at any time, and gradually we began to experience some kind of thrill at the storm's violence.

When the ship pitched it was quite thrilling and we found we could have quite exciting times attempting to walk on deck, and had to hang on for dear life when sailing into the wind.

One day, Miss Mousley, feeling a little adventurous, asked me if I would take her around the prow of the ship; more than for any other reason, I suspected, to have something other than the rail to hang onto. So, with this challenge I agreed, and off we went, hanging onto the rail and each other and pulling ourselves towards the front whilst the ship's steel cables were screaming in the wind. With much endeavour, we made it to the prow, only to find it was much more difficult putting on the brakes to come back again, though we did accomplish it without harm, but it certainly was quite an adventure, and one I expect the young lady would remember.

We had been at sea for about two and a half days when our sailing chart signified that we were exactly half way across the Atlantic Ocean.

'The Professor' suggested that he and I went through to the tourist class to partake of an evening's entertainment. There was dancing and a very nice bar, so we had a couple of drinks and the occasional dance. There were quite a few Mexicans among the passengers and we had not been there much more than half an hour when a foreign gentleman approached me, as I was thanking a lady for having danced with me, and said, "Excuse me, but are you not a first class passenger?"

"Yes" I said,

"Well go and dance with your own ladies."

He obviously thought I had ulterior motives, and so to retreat seemed the better part of valour, as we could not afford to be involved. 'The Professor' had already sensed the position and we took our leave soon afterwards.

The storm lasted over two days and there were very heavy seas, but at that moment in time we were ignorant of the fact that the ship had been engaged in a distress call and that we had gone over 100 miles off course in answer to an SOS signal. This particular piece of information I learned only after the trip was over and my wife asked me, in London, if it was exciting going to the rescue of a ship at sea. I was unaware of anything of the kind happening, but the newspapers had reported the incident. The *Europa's* assistance was not actually required, as some other ship had arrived on the scene.

When the storm abated, we were able to continue with other activities. Playing deck quoits, using the rifle-range and walking around the ship, generally studying the other passengers which was a very interesting pastime, and we would spend long spells just watching the wake of this great ship, which stretched almost to the horizon.

The days passed very quickly and we began to search the distance for signs of land. Yes, over there on our starboard side was Long Island. We glided closer and closer to terra firma and soon, looking down upon us on our left was the great Statue of Liberty. However, I had other things to think about as well.

Our luggage must be in a state of readiness and I had to attend, also, to The Hon Esmond's packing as well as that of Master Vere's and my own. 'The Professor' and Miss Mousley had discussed these final arrangements as all our luggage would have to be kept together whilst leaving the boat and passing through the customs officials. In our case, this exercise was made considerably easier. Viscount Rothermere, being a well-known traveller and also a great Statesman, would, of course, with his party, leave the ship at the earliest opportunity, to be whisked away to their respective hotels, leaving the staff, in this case, 'The Professor', Miss Mousley and myself, to follow on with the luggage. We were, it seemed, also privileged in as much as we had all our pieces of luggage marked with a cross, so that when we arrived at the point in Customs where passengers passed through in alphabetical order, we were very speedily dispensed with, and in no time at all were through the formalities and free to leave.

Soon we had our various pieces of luggage placed in waiting taxicabs and instructed the drivers to take us to the Plaza Hotel. We were speedily whisked along the waterfront and into New York, and before very long we had arrived at the hotel. Porters then took over and had the appropriate luggage sorted and dispatched to the allotted appointments.

We were all on the sixteenth floor where His Lordship had a private suite, and when I was taken to my own quarters, I found I was installed in a lovely room with twin beds and adjacent was a private bathroom.

"Oh what a waste!" was the thought that went through my mind. A honeymoon situation with no bride to share my perfect quarters. Nevertheless, I must enjoy my splendid solitary confinement.

Before I could settle down for the night however, I had to see and arrange the well-being of Master Vere who had a room in Lord Rothermere's suite. Before very long I had unpacked his belongings, got him some light refreshment as it was getting late, and got him tucked up for the night. This seemed the right thing to do, and these little duties attended to I returned to my own quarters once more. The chambermaid came to see me and asked what time I should be called and did I need an early morning tea-tray. Having sorted out these details to my liking, she took her leave.

Being alone at last, I decided that before retiring for the night, I would investigate 'The Professor's' whereabouts, and I eventually contacted him. He had finished with His Lordship for the night, so we took the lift downstairs and discovered that there was a special couriers' room for the servants of the elite. We partook of sandwiches and a glass of beer and after a chat about the events of the day, decided to go to bed.

I was awakened at 8 o'clock in the morning to the music of the china being placed on the bedside table. It was a beautiful day and as I looked out of my window overlooking Central Park, there was a grand view which needed to be seen to be appreciated.

Having completed my toilet, I made my way once more to the couriers' room where breakfast was being served. 'The Professor' and Miss Mousley were already partaking of theirs. I ordered my own, talking the while of the general situation. 'The Professor' having finished his meal, left to attend to His Lordship's needs, but to our surprise, he was back soon afterwards. He said the Old Man wanted to see me right away, so I hurriedly made for the lift to the sixteenth floor and knocked on His Lordship's door. "Come in laddie."

"Good morning, My Lord."

"Well what do you think of New York?"

"I am most impressed, and can't wait to see as much as I can," I told him.

"Well Chinnock, I have a job for you to look after Master Vere for me. This is his first visit to New York and it's up to you to see that he never forgets it. You must take great care of him, and I don't want him to be kidnapped. You understand that it's an important duty I am asking you to do. You know what a young man likes to do!"

"Yes, My Lord, like Madison Square Gardens, the Circus, the Empire State Building and...."

"Yes, you have the right ideas, you can report to me each evening when you put him to bed, and let me know what you get up to."

"Yes, thank you My Lord."

"Now money …-"

"I have money, My Lord." but he reached into his pocket book and presented me with 200 dollars.

"You will need plenty, and I'll give you 200 dollars each morning, and be sure Master Vere enjoys himself!"

I thought I was in fairyland, what a commission this was! At that time, there were five dollars to the pound. I took my leave of His Lordship and joined Master Vere in his room. From this point on, I am not required to resort to the couriers' room for my meals, because I should be dining with Master Vere and would therefore use the hotel's dining room.

I first took Master Vere to the foyer where we found particulars of all the theatres and amusements. We browsed around and decided what we would do. We booked tickets for the shows of our choice, and charged them to Viscount Rothermere's account. It was simplicity itself. We then went out into the city of New York and hailed a yellow taxicab and our adventures began. I asked the taxi man to take us for a general run around the city, 5th, 6th and 7th Avenues and Broadway and Wall Street. I was interested to note that in the cab was a registration document, with a photograph of the driver and I thought that a very good idea. One felt more secure being able to check the driver with his picture. I remember we went to the Woolworth Building, Trinity Church then to Mr Jack Dempsey's restaurant, where I paid the taxi man off and we stayed for a meal. I was personally interested, because being fond of boxing I had seen Gene Tunney take the championship in 1926 (on film of course) for the world title, whilst I was still a boy.

Having satisfied our appetites, we called another cab and went to Madison Square Garden where there was a grand circus to see. I don't recall how many ice-cream sodas we consumed but I know we were getting a great liking for them. The circus was a great success. Before we entered the actual arena where our seats were, there was a series of sideshows, the India-rubber Man, the Wild Man from Borneo, etc. We were both most intrigued, and it was whilst I was looking intently at the sword swallower whose stomach was behind an X-Ray screen where the sword could be seen moving up and down, that I turned to say something to Master Vere and he wasn't there. Thoughts of Al Capone and kidnappers filled my mind and instantly I shouted loudly "Vere!" I was so relieved to see his head appear from around the gentleman I was standing next to. "Yes," he said and looked askance at my behaviour, and he wasn't the only one. I'm sure people thought I must have a screw loose or something. But I was so grateful to be able to shepherd him into his seat as the circus performance was about to take place, and I then recapped the horrible experience and the 'what might have been', and settled down beside Vere to watch. Having by now recovered a little from my shock I was able to concentrate on the performance which was, I remember, excellent.

During the interval, the vendors came with popcorn, ice cream and all manner of goodies on trays for our pleasure. One man came with a basket of live chameleons – people were buying them so I bought one to examine more closely. It had the power of rapidly changing colour according to its surroundings. Master Vere was quite interested in watching it, as it harmonised with the colour of anything it was placed upon. After having satisfied our curiosity and learning that they were natives of Africa and/or Madagascar, I thought it discrete to return it to the vendor as I was at a loss to know what else to do with it – it would hardly have been welcomed at the Plaza Hotel.

We also enjoyed the second part of the circus, and at the end of the performance, we walked again past the various sideshows out onto the sidewalk. I kept a keen eye on Master Vere, my shock still being uppermost in my mind. We were getting hooked on soda fountain bars and as soon as we saw the next one we entered to sample their concoctions. We found a pineapple grove alongside this soda bar, most tastefully decorated with pineapples of choice quality and the most delicious pineapple drinks served with ice cream. Having sampled and enjoyed our refreshment we passed on to the other things, and finding a rifle range we took a turn at shooting. We had got used to using the rifle range on the boat, so when or wherever we saw a rifle range we were happy to indulge to see who would get the best target results.

A day spent 'on the loose' in New York had gone all too quickly, and certainly our first day disappeared like magic. I called a yellow cab and we went back to our hotel. With a tired but happy young man by my side, I mentally summarised my report on the day's activities which His Lordship was most interested to discuss with me later.

Each day was wonderful, the weather perfect. We spent a day at the Bronx Zoo going there by taxicab – in fact, we did all our trips by this method. We must have travelled many miles in and around New York City. We were able to see the different walks of life, such as the youngsters playing baseball in the back streets, and no doubt, they would be hoping to be 'greats' like the current hero Babe Ruth.

On one occasion, whilst on our way to visit the Empire State Building, we had been commenting on the big Irish policeman at the intersections and were very much amused with the backchat between the taxi drivers and the policemen. Our taxi driver pointed upwards and remarked, "There look, that's the Empire State Building peeping above the mist." As we both followed his pointing finger, he suddenly stood on his brakes and stopped at an intersection with such emergency that Master Vere and I were hurled forward in the cab, both cracking our heads and putting us in a most uncomfortable position. The cabby was sorry. I had a bumped forehead and Master Vere had a nosebleed but all in all we were none the worse for wear and by the time we alighted at the Empire State Building we had recovered our dignity, at least, and looked forward to what lay ahead.

1. Harold Sidney Harmsworth, 1st Viscount Rothermere (26 April 1868 26 November 1940) at Gleneagles on 4th September 1931

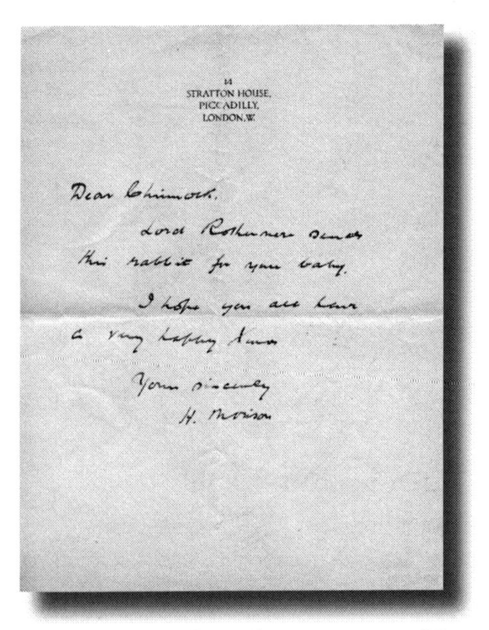

14
STRATTON HOUSE,
PICCADILLY,
LONDON, W.

Dear Chinnock,

Lord Rothermere sends this rabbit for your baby.

I hope you all have a very happy time

Yours sincerely
H. Morison

2. Letter referred to on page 98

3. Piper for a day

4. Plus fours in Dornoch

5. Fun in the garden

6. With Judy

7. With Fletch

8. The author with his wife Fletch and staff in the gardens of Burghfield House, Dornoch

9. Masseur walking on the left of King Carol II of Romania in the funeral procession of King George V

10. Master Vere aged 10

11. Stody Lodge in the 1930s from the front

12. and from the back

13. Stody Lodge from the air

14. The view from the terrace

15. Stody Lodge – The Front Hall and staircase

16. The Front Hall

17. Stody Lodge – The Drawing Room

18. Drawing Room Fireplace

19. Stody Lodge – The Dining Room

20. Dining Room
Adam Fireplace

The walls of this room were lined with honeysuckle bark!

21. The Orange Seller 22. The Tinder Seller

These two *Cries of London* prints hung on the staircase in the Front Hall

23. Mrs Morison with Mr & Mrs F.J.Clark

24. The Hon Esmond Harmsworth introducing Sir Donald Campbell at a banquet in London honouring his speed triumphs.

# Upstairs downstairs life 'a fairytale'

A life among the aristocracy in 1930s Britain has been detailed by a Bognor Regis man in his autobiography.

Wilf Chinnock, aged 80, was butler to newspaper magnate Viscount Rothermere for about eight years until the outbreak of World War Two.

Working for the man whose family owned - and still owns the Daily Mail and associated papers - brought Mr Chinnock into contact with many of that era's leading public figures.

Daily Express owner Lord Beaverbrook, war-time leader Winston Churchill, the German ambassador in London, Herr von Ribbentrop, and Liberal prime minister David Lloyd-George were among the famous personalities Mr Chinnock met.

Mr Chinnock enjoyed his time as his servant after joining the Rothermere staff when he left his Somerset home to work in London.

His wife, Fletch (80), was a parlour maid in the households. She said Viscount Rothermere treated his staff very well despite the 'upstairs downstairs' regime.

COLOURFUL MEMORIES: Retired butler Wilf Chinnock (80), with his autobiography, which includes memories of Lord Rothermere. - Photo sales no. 7230-1.

Mr Chinnock joined the Royal Army Service Corps when the Second World War began. At the end of the conflict, he was on the first convoy into a liberated Berlin.

He and his wife came to Bognor after the war to run the Primrose Cafe next to the Picturedrome and work in an hotel. Mr Chinncok then worked at Hago and Lec Refrigeration.

The couple have lived in their present town centre home for 46 years. They have two daughters, seven grandchildren and ten great-grandchildren.

Mr Chinnock said: "My book reads like a fairytale. People say it didn't really happen but it did. It was our life."

25. The Bognor Regis Observer 11th February 1993

We entered the lift and were soon speeding upwards at what seemed an incredible rate. My ears were ringing and Vere had the same sensation, so we were both glad to arrive at the top, but had we – no! We still had another lift to complete the journey. However, we did eventually arrive and we were very impressed with what we saw. People and traffic below looked like a concourse of ants and no place to be for persons with no head for heights. We met a guide who gave us a few local details, and apologised for it not being a clear day – the visibility being only twenty-five miles that day. He also told us that in really bad weather the top of the building actually swayed.

We took our leave after a while, and alighting from the lift after the first part of the descent we discovered a restaurant, but decided not to stay as we had a full programme on that day, so we returned to the Plaza Hotel for lunch. It was a great occasion for me to be able to go into this splendid dining room, with swaying palms and soft sweet music amongst the elite of society. As the head waiter shepherded us to our table I was aware of the looks of approval we were receiving from various directions and I wondered what these elegant personages might be thinking, as I could so easily have passed for Vere's father, I being then twenty-six years of age and Master Vere being then 12 years old. However, one thing was for sure, we both enjoyed our lunch and played our parts with dignity.

In the afternoon, we went to the Roxy Theatre, the largest, I believe, in New York. I fail to recall the pictures we saw but I do remember that Rudy Vallée came on stage in the interval and sang "*Tipi, Tipi Tin.*"

I was interested in card manipulation and had shown Master Vere a few of my tricks and had also bought a book called *Blackstone's Modern Card Tricks*. We had quite a lot of fun with various magic illusions I came across. One evening as we returned to the hotel we met His Lordship in his sitting room.

"Hello Chinnock and what have you been up to today? Oh, and by the way, Master Vere tells me you do wonderful things with cards and I would like you to show them to me."

"Yes, My Lord." So with my illustrious employer poised watching my every move, I produced a pack of playing cards and, with a silent prayer that I would acquit myself in a worthy manner, I did my four best tricks and really enjoyed the atmosphere that prevailed. His Lordship congratulated me on my dexterity and asked me if I could teach Master Vere. I replied that of course I could. His Lordship thought it would be great for a young man like Vere to be able to come up with something like that when attending a party.

Master Vere was a very lively young man and soon wanted to know when he could begin to wear evening dress. I told him it would bc sooner than he imagined. His sister, Miss Lorna, had been having some spending sprees, and Master Vere wanted to know when he would be able to have lots of money to spend. I told him he would one day; in fact, as he would be the future Viscount Rothermere he would have nothing to worry about, and would be able to spend all the money he wanted to. “Will I really?” he said.

When I suggested it was time for bed, he wanted to know what the hurry was; was it that I intended to take Miss Mousley to the International Casino, as he had heard her talking about it. I told him that she may be going but certainly not with me, and that the only reason I suggested his going to bed was that it was his bedtime.

Each day was a brand new thrill for me; we did so many things and visited so many wonderful places. The Planetarium, for instance, was something we both enjoyed, the little church around the corner, Wall Street, a walk in Central Park – all were lovely – and every day we had 200 dollars to spend. We visited fun fairs and soda bars to our hearts content.

One day we came across some terrapin turtles in a pet shop, with their shells beautifully glazed in various colours and tiny etched pictures of Popeye, Shirley Temple, Mickey Mouse, Olive Oil, Pluto, and so forth. These delighted Master Vere and he said we must buy some, so we purchased about a dozen. I had mentioned that I didn’t think we could take them to the hotel, but he was sure it would be alright as he could keep them in the bathroom. I replied that we should have to keep it a secret and that we should require to buy some food for them. So Master Vere enjoyed his new found friends and I had another responsibility.

One evening after I had put Master Vere to bed, I was on my way through His Lordship's suite when he asked what I had been up to today. I was about to relate my daily programme when into the sitting room came Miss Lorna looking an absolute picture as though she had stepped out of a fashion magazine.

His Lordship said, "Hello, my dear, you look very lovely; and where, may I ask, are you going this evening?"

"I'm going to the theatre Grand-dad." she exclaimed.

"And whom might you be going with?" At this point Miss Lorna mentioned a young man's name – "Oh no you are not, I forbid you to go." said His Lordship.

"But I want to go to the theatre." she said.

At this point, His Lordship looked at me and turning to Miss Lorna once more said, "If you have set your heart on going to the theatre, you may go but Chinnock will be your chaperon."

"I'm not going with him!" she replied.

"Very well, then you can't go at all."

Eventually however she looked at me and said, "Oh very well, come along then." So after a very quick change I was off in a taxicab with a most beautiful young person – I think she may have been about seventeen at the time – and as fashionable as Fifth Avenue could turn out. I was indeed very proud to have the opportunity of escorting The Hon Lorna Harmsworth to a theatre in New York City. Later in life, this young lady married Sir Neill Cooper-Key and I feel very proud of my association with so many very famous personalities. The evening at the theatre was a memorable one.

Next morning Master Vere and I were off on another jaunt. I did keep a round account of expenses, but this was totally unnecessary. I suggested we buy His Lordship an Easter present, and took Master Vere into a very nice florist shop where we ordered an appropriate bouquet. It was, I remember, a trelliswork with a large teddy bear, arranged together with masses of choice blooms. I believe I have already mentioned in this book how passionately fond of flowers His Lordship was. Having arranged for their delivery, we set off once more on our adventures. Our time was now getting short as we were to leave New York on 20th April 1938.

I remember getting everything packed and ready for our departure, and I asked Master Vere what we should do about our terrapins. We had managed to keep them in the bathroom for several days. I didn't think we would be allowed to take them on board, but Master Vere thought we would, so on the sailing date we took our new found friends with us aboard RMS *Aquitania* and at our earliest opportunity popped them in the cabin sink partly filled with water and hoped for the best. 'The Professor', His Lordship, Miss Lorna, Miss Mousley, and The Hon Esmond Harmsworth were now aboard and Mr Esmond was pleased to see his son. He had been on business whilst in New York and we had therefore seen very little of him. He was keen to know how Vere had enjoyed himself.

Two days before we boarded was my wife's birthday, 18th April, I sent a Western Union cablegram:

***Birthday Greetings Darling stop. Leaving Wednesday midday Love Wilf***

Incidentally, 20th April 1938, the day we boarded the ship, was our wedding anniversary.

RMS *Aquitania* was a four-funnel ship with a quadruple screw and a gross tonnage of 45,647 and belonged to the Cunard White Star Line, a comfortable ship; and so we departed from New York with all the excitement she had afforded us still fresh in our memories, but we soon slipped back into the routine of life aboard.

On the following morning, I happened to meet Lord Rothermere taking his constitutional around the deck. "Good morning, Chinnock." he said.

"Good morning, My Lord." I replied.

"Walk with me for a while I want to talk to you."

"Yes, My Lord."

"Well, firstly I would thank you very much indeed for looking after Master Vere, he has enjoyed himself immensely, and I have been thinking about those card tricks you performed. When we get back to London I will engage the services of the finest magician possible, to teach you the rudiments, and you can then pass on what you learn to Master Vere. What do you think of that, does it appeal to you?"

"Yes, thank you My Lord, it will be a thrilling experience."

"Very well, and another thing, Master Vere will be having his summer holidays next and I will advise you of the dates later on. When you get back to London you can organise something with Thomas Cook, and I will furnish you with travellers' cheques. Sort out a nice cruise and you can take Master Vere and another young man from Eton for a companion. We will talk about it again."

I took my leave of him with so much elation I didn't know what to do next, so I just contemplated for a few minutes as I looked at the sea romping by and wondered was there anyone as lucky as myself.

I then went off to find Master Vere again and, as I did so, I thought I would keep His Lordship's confidence. He didn't say I couldn't mention it to Vere, but at the same time I thought that if His Lordship chose to mention our plans he was at liberty to do so, but that I would keep it a surprise until further developments. I had lots of things to tell my wife about our adventures.

When I found Master Vere, he had unhappy news to relate. Two of our terrapins had died; I feared that we should lose them all, so I told him not to get upset, as I had explained at the outset that I had been doubtful of their survival. So Shirley Temple and Mickey Mouse had to be buried. I suggested a burial at sea and arranged a little chute for the purpose of sliding them overboard, and we arranged a little goodbye service quickly thought up. Unhappily, they all eventually were likewise dispatched.

There was lots of fun and games to be had on board, so we soon had happier things to do and forgot our sorrow for our pets.

On some occasions, Master Vere would join his family for a while. One early evening he came and met me on deck. "Look what I've got!" he cried excitedly and showed me quite a few pound notes, ten or twelve maybe.

"Oh Vere, where did you get all that money?"

"I won it playing Lotto or Housey, Housey or some such game."

I was so happy for him, but I must have shown too much enthusiasm for I said, "What a lot of money to win, you are a lucky boy." and of course, £10 was quite a tidy sum in those days. However, he looked at me as I congratulated him on his win and, with a very serious face, he said, "I want you to have it Chinnock." and held out his hand towards me.

"You know I can't accept this Master Vere, don't you?"

"Oh yes, you can, I'd like you to."

"No, Master Vere, I think you are very kind and I do appreciate your intention, but I have a jolly good idea, we will spend it together, it's your grandfather's birthday on the 26th April so let's go shopping on the ship in the morning for a present for him." He readily agreed and we found ourselves the next morning browsing around the shops and we finally decided on a porcelain salmon trout paperweight.

"His Lordship will love that Master Vere, and we can make our presentation on the ship, as on the 26th we will be arriving at Southampton," I said.

All too soon we crossed the Atlantic ocean and before very long we had entered Southampton Water, where the ship discharged its bilge tanks – not a pretty sight, but the seagulls were evidently delighted as they wheeled and dived and screamed as long as the effluence continued, gobbling up all except the wooden crates, cardboard boxes and paper which left an untidy mess in the wake of the big ship. Soon there was peace and quiet as we left the noisy chorus in the distance.

I once more prepared to leave the ship and finished packing our belongings and soon we were docking and all our assortment of luggage was once again rounded up together and we waited to disembark.

We had made the presentation for His Lordship's birthday and Master Vere was obviously pleased with the way in which it was received, the paperweight would certainly not be out of place on His Lordship's desk.

All too soon, it was time to say goodbye to Master Vere, as he would be travelling back to London with The Hon Esmond Harmsworth's party, and I was therefore dismissed. Having said goodbye to Miss Lorna and her maid, I searched out 'The Professor' again and together we found the train which His Lordship had already boarded.

Future plans were forming in my mind. My wife and baby were waiting for me at Stratton House and I had much to tell my wife of my adventures, and I had so many pleasant things to think about my future. I had brought presents from New York, was happy to be back in England, and could hardly wait to rejoin my family once more. How the baby had grown in twenty days, I was quite surprised at her progress.

We were soon having more well-known personalities at Stratton House once again, calling for interviews with Lord Rothermere. However, I lost no time at all in going around to Thomas Cook in Berkeley Street, to arrange for the coming summer holidays with Master Vere. After lots of advice from the travel agent, I thought we might very well enjoy a trip to Spitsbergen, it sounded so exciting. So I took some brochures of the *SS Atlantis*, with the understanding that I would be in touch as soon as our plans developed, and, of course, I was still looking forward to meeting a magician who would instruct me. The following weeks passed very quickly.

About this time Lord Rothermere had presented to Edward (Teddy) Fells, who had been his valet for thirty years, and to F.J.Clark, who was one of his secretaries, and also had thirty years' service, a gold inscribed wrist watch each from Cartier's of Bond Street. I say this now as I have to introduce Edward Fells again, because for the preceding year or so His Lordship had left Teddy in charge of his house, Stody Lodge, in Norfolk and had more or less had his masseur George Honour to accompany him on all his travels, leaving Teddy to run the household in Norfolk. Teddy had been a life long friend of Jimmy Clark who, incidentally, paid the accounts for all the households of Viscount Rothermere. Jimmy Clark had recently pointed out to me an account from Findlater Mackie Todd saying that he couldn't think what Teddy was up to, running up such costs as he had had no guests there for at least a couple of months. He said he kept covering up as much as possible, but felt he must consult His Lordship concerning this account.

## Chapter XIII

# DISPATCHED TO STODY LODGE

**EVENTUALLY I WAS SUMMONED** by His Lordship, who said he wanted me to take over the house in Norfolk. He thought that anyway I would be better off there than in London when the bombs started to fall. I asked him if he thought the war was that near, and he replied that anyone who doesn't think so is an imbecile. He suggested that I had a word with my wife, which I did, and His Lordship rang to ask if we had made up our minds. On hearing that we had, he said that Clark would drive with me, that the chauffeur was waiting and that Rose could follow at a later date.

So, within ten minutes, I had left Stratton House forever, all because Teddy had been overloading the wine bill and hitting the bottle in the most spectacular way. It proved to be a blessing in disguise for us and Lord Rothermere had been right about a war very soon to commence.

Edward Fells was retired at £5 a week for life. I hope he enjoyed his retirement; he lived in Christchurch near Bournemouth with his wife and family.

On arrival at Stody Lodge, Melton Constable, Norfolk I was introduced, by F.J.Clark, to the staff. The house itself was on the small side; it had been purposely built so that His Lordship would have an ideal excuse for not having too many houseguests. Actually, it housed more staff than guests, and the sleeping accommodation included Lord Rothermere's bedroom and just four other principal bedrooms. The staff comprised, housekeeper, three housemaids, four kitchen staff, two footmen, one pantry boy and myself, as from then.

'The Garage', which was situated on the other side of the road down a beautifully lined rhododendron drive, could accommodate six chauffeurs with staff for feeding facilities, and a private petrol tank which was replenished at regular intervals by the garage man, who lived at Holt. I was to take over Gate Lodge, which stood nearby, which would also accommodate two footmen. We had a home farm with our own dairy herd adjacent to a Guest House where we lodged the overflow when we had shooting parties. We had a most excellent shoot, three gamekeepers and an estate manager, who lived in a house next to the garages.

Opposite was a most beautiful azalea garden with little oriental wooden bridges criss-crossing tiny waterways, with an occasional magnolia tree on tiny islands. It was a veritable picture and was surrounded by tall pine trees. It was a basin of colour and perfume to the visitor – a sight to be remembered. When at its prime, it was opened to the public, who came from miles around to see it and pay their one-shilling entrance fee which was collected on behalf of a deserving charity.

The garage buildings and the surrounding property were the site of the original Stody Lodge. All were placed in the most advantageous site and built to existing conditions. Many old trees were incorporated into the designing of the new creation, the pleasure gardens of which were tended by seven gardeners.

The lawns were first class, having been laid by Suttons of Reading. The gardeners' cottages lay alongside the road leading to Holt, they were indeed ornate, and were thatched with Norfolk reeds. Opposite stretched an enormous fruit farm full of the most choice strawberries, raspberries, black and red currants, and a huge store house, also thatched with Norfolk reeds, and with a most imposing aspect.

I think the story was that His Lordship was at one stage going to have pigs installed, with porcelain walls in grand style but it was brought to his notice that his pigs would be living in better conditions than the local inhabitants, and so the idea was scrapped and the building became a super store for Cox's apples and other choice fruits. Down near the home farm were the glasshouses in which were grown cantaloupe melons, muscatel grapes, blue grapes and even pineapples, tomatoes and the most perfect houseplants and flowers always available in season.

The pheasant shoot was one of the best. I never discovered the acreage of the estate, but we had about ten tenant farmers and I realised, when shooting or walking abroad that I would be most unlikely to walk off the estate. There was a trout stream which His Lordship had had stocked with salmon trout, and our immediate neighbour was the Lord Hastings.

I had a grand pantry, a great kitchen and scullery, an outside boots department and several outhouses for kindling etc.

There were also woodmen who felled trees when necessary and kept the house supplied with logs for the whole of the winter months. The staff hall was quite a nice large room which seated twelve to the table, and there was a wireless set as well. We were on the mains for the electricity supply but the Guest House had its own generator which needed constant attention when we had guests to cater for.

I had lots to do and a responsibility, but on 13th May 1938, I received the following letter from the Grand Hotel, Des Iles Borromees, Stresa – Borromeo:

***Dear Chinnock,***

***The following instructions are from His Lordship:***

***So far as possible you must use in the house only vegetables that are grown in the garden, and I am writing to Mr Goude to see that you get all you want. Flowers for the house must not be bought; these must also come from the gardens. With regard to vegetables, you should occasionally walk around the gardens so that you will know what to order.***

***Keep a record of all the vegetables with which Mr Goude supplies you. His Lordship will, from time to time, ask you to show it to him. You understand, of course, that you are in charge of the house and that you and nobody else will give the house staff their orders.***

*Write to me at the Grand Hotel, Venice, saying you have received this letter.*

*Yours sincerely,*

*H.Morison*

Mr Harry Goude mentioned in the letter was the estate manager. I was gradually getting myself organised, but was, at the same time, having a little difficulty with Christina, the housekeeper. We were not seeing eye to eye at this time. She had raised an objection when I had asked her to hand over certain keys which she had in her possession, and she had handed them over to me rather reluctantly. Then on the 20th June 1938 I received the following letter from Stratton House:

*Dear Chinnock,*

*Apparently, Christina is not finding her position as comfortable as formerly*
*Try to straighten things out so that the organisation of Stody Lodge runs smoothly and efficiently. It might be a good thing if you had a quiet chat with her. She is an old and trusted servant and your job will be easier if you are working amicably together. I have written to her telling her that you are responsible for the good organisation of Stody Lodge.*
*I am quite sure with your tact that you will settle this problem so that Christina does not feel she has a grievance. As you know, His Lordship expects his establishments to be run quietly and efficiently and I am sure you can do it.*

*Yours very faithfully,*

*H.Morison*

I did try to resolve our differences on the strength of this letter but unhappily, Christina eventually decided that she would not work under my supervision and very shortly afterwards decided to leave His Lordship's employ. She was replaced by Miss Kathleen Ponting, who came from the house in Avenue Road where she was principally ladiesmaid for Miss Judith Wilson, a daughter of one of Lord

Rothermere's cousins, Mrs Adelaide Wilson – both these ladies were quite frequent visitors to Stody Lodge.

Mr Esmond Harmsworth often came for a shoot, bringing his own guests. Lady O'Neal was frequently in his party around this time with other distinguished guests. I did not have a shooting room at the Lodge but instead there was a very large cupboard which housed the guns and ammunition boxes. These house parties went with a swing – only the best was good enough for His Lordship's guests, and the finest wines were available at all times.

It was a lovely sight to see the shooting party take their leave for a day's shooting. There would be twenty to thirty beaters to drive the game, and a day's bag could be 250-300 brace of pheasants, two or three hares and the odd rabbit or so. The day's bag was taken care of by the head gamekeeper who kept a huge game larder; everyone could eat a whole pheasant for dinner if so desired. The staff hall never went short at any time. We used to have pheasant the first night of the shoot when fresh, otherwise a week after hanging, when we could have them from the gamekeeper.

The Hon Esmond Harmsworth's party usually stayed for a week or so and the staff would all do their utmost to see that they were well looked after. The evening meal was always very carefully prepared by the kitchen staff, and always finished with dessert, liqueur, cigarettes or cigars (double coronas, always) and brandy. Some of the ladies occasionally brought their maids, and sometimes a valet would have to be catered for.

The last duty for each day was to prepare the 'grog' tray, a huge oval silver tray with an assortment of drinks, to which the household could help themselves. After this, all the staff could retire.

If Mr Esmond chose to play cards, and he often did, it was usually Bezique or Bridge, then I would be the one to remain to make sure everything was secure after everyone had gone to bed. So, sometimes I was on duty at 6 a.m. and it could be 1 a.m. before I was finished. However, these stints were of short duration, I could find myself, the following week 'King of the Castle' with nobody in residence, and I was left to my own devices.

When I left Stratton House, it was early May 1938 and my wife joined me in early July. In the meantime, I had been measuring the accommodation we were to take over, for carpets, curtains, etc and supplying my wife with the room sizes.

We had no furniture as yet, so we arranged for the complete furnishing over the 'phone. And on the appointed day, to coincide with the arrival of my wife and babe, came a pantechnicon from The Cavendish Furniture Co Ltd., Oxford Street, London W.l., the contents of which was as follows (and it might be interesting to cost these items):

| | | |
|---|---|---|
| **1** | **Three Piece Walnut Bedroom suite, comprising:** | |
| | **Tallboy, Dressing table, Wardrobe** | **£25.10s.0d.** |
| **1** | **Walnut Bed to match** | **£30. 0s.0d.** |
| **1** | **4'6" Spring interior mattress & base** | **£ 5.14s.6d.** |
| **1** | **Walnut dining Room suite, comprising:** | |
| | **Table, 4 chairs and sideboard** | **£16.16s.0d.** |
| **3** | **Carpets** | **£14. 0s.0d.** |
| **3** | **Under felts** | **£2.15s.0d.** |
| **1** | **China cabinet** | **£3. 5s.0d.** |
| **1** | **Nest of tables (gratis)** | |
| | | **£98. 0s.0d.** |
| **Less £1 0s 0d deposit** | | **£ 1. 0s.0d.** |
| | | **£97. 0s.0d.** |
| | | **=======** |

My wife had purchased cutlery, curtains, and all the other household knickknacks from Selfridges, and we had many willing hands to install us in our new abode. My wife was not working now, so would be able to take her leisure with our baby daughter. In consequence, I received the following letter from F.J.Clark:

**14**
**STRATTON HOUSE**
**PICCADILLY,**
**LONDON W.**

***Dear Chinnock,***

***I have been instructed to inform you that your wages as from the week ending July 2nd next, will be reduced to £3.0s.0d. (three pounds a week)***

***Yours truly,***

***F.J.Clark.***

So my wage was reduced but my overall situation was improved considerably, in kind. Free housing, heating, electric light, and although I had had that in London, all garden produce was to be supplied to my wife including – well, just anything. The gardener called on her every morning to know her requirements. Peaches, nectarines, strawberries, vegetables, anything in season were available at all times and I could shoot and fish to my hearts delight, and fill our little home with flowers anytime – and what flowers!

Mr Harry Morison, financial secretary to His Lordship, possessed a Remington Repeating .22 rifle and gave me verbal permission to use it whenever I liked. The first year I used three thousand rounds of .22 ammo., but thereby hangs a tale which I think I should relate a little later on in my story.

Stody and Hunworth were two small parishes, and one Padre officiated at the two small churches. Lord Rothermere had invited the Padre to lunch on one occasion and during the after-lunch conversation, the Padre had told His Lordship of the shocking condition of one of his church roofs – there had obviously been difficulty in finance, and His Lordship said:

"Well Padre, don't worry yourself about it any more, why don't you just get your church roof re-leaded and send me the bill."

The Padre was most profuse with his thanks. I just mentioned this as one instance of Viscount Rothermere's great generosity and kindness. On the other hand, he could be equally shrewd when the situation warranted.

When he decided to spend some time at Stody, I would be notified by the secretary, a day's notice, usually, and then it was 'action stations'. The garden and greenhouse staff were alerted, and the house would then be invaded with pot plants and flowers of all descriptions. There was a special flower arranging area with stone floors, and surrounded by cupboards and shelves that housed a lovely selection of vases of different shapes and sizes. I took charge of the arranging part of the operation myself, but with such exotic flowers, my task was not only a great pleasure, but a labour of love.

It is difficult to make mistakes when everything that comes to hand is of the choicest, and that, of course refers also to food and wine, and immaculate table linen. Everyone worked with a will, and by the time His Lordship was due to arrive, everyone was on parade. Two footmen were standing with me in the hall dressed in undress livery and I, myself, was in full morning dress and on alert.

Bob Tanner, the head chauffeur, who would be driving His Lordship in his Rolls 50, knew the drill. As he entered the avenue of trees, about five hundred yards down the roadway, he would give a blast on his hooter, so that when the car turned into the house drive proper, the door would be standing wide open, a footman on either side of the outside steps, with myself on the threshold waiting to welcome His Lordship, where he would be received in a fashion to which he was accustomed.

If he chose to walk past us with not as much as a word – and he often did just that – nobody would interrupt his train of thought, for he could have affairs of state on his mind and might walk straight past us across the hall and through the drawing room to the French windows and out onto the pleasure garden which was almost in a direct line from the front door and take a leisurely stroll by himself, but this was not always the case.

Sometimes he would stop and say, "Hello Chinnock, how is your wife and baby?" and then talk quite freely of things which interested him. He would ask what sort of bird life we had in our vicinity. On this occasion, I replied that there was a great spotted woodpecker nesting in the nesting box under the garden wall. He found that interesting and asked to see it. I said, "I doubt whether Your Lordship could spare the time as they are very furtive birds, but I will endeavour to show you one of the young ones before they finally leave the nest." He enquired if we had any more interesting birds in the pleasure gardens.

"Yes, My Lord," I replied "garden warblers and goldcrests."

"Why don't you walk in the garden with me and introduce me to a few of your feathered friends?"

And this I did, and was able to show him a few nests, with which he was highly delighted.

He then said, "Tell me Chinnock, how many species of bird life would you think might be on an area say a mile square on the Estate?"

"That's a tricky question" I replied, "but off-hand I would say 85."

"Do you really mean that Chinnock"?

"Well you asked me, and that's my personal estimation."

This particular episode must have lingered in his mind because at a later date, maybe two months later, on another visit to Stody, he made my day for he came up to me and said, "Chinnock I have to congratulate you. I had my birdman from the *Daily Mail* to make a census on the bird life down here and he tells me there are 90 different species – so you were not so far wrong – good for you!"

For me, Stody was a blissful place, quite idyllic in fact and, shortly after I took up duties there I was instructed to organise a celebration tea party to include strawberries and cream, to honour the occasion of King George VI and Queen Elizabeth's Coronation. All the estate personnel, the Padre and his wife and all the children of the two parishes of Hunworth and Stody were to be invited.

Lord Rothermere was always most generous and loved to help in any way, where children were concerned.

Each Christmas he would instruct his agent to have three full-grown Christmas trees to be cut from his estate. One would be erected on the village green, one on the platform of Melton Constable Railway Station and the third outside Stody Lodge. All of these would be dressed with Christmas tree lights for the benefit of the observers.

While I am on the subject of Christmas, I will relate some of the happenings. To begin with, the Padre and his wife and myself would organise a Christmas party and festival for the children of the two parishes. Each child was to be the recipient of a present which was, in time, to hang on another Christmas tree inside the village hall. A grand tea party was also organised by the staff from Stody Lodge and in the meantime, we made notes of all the children's names who would be attending the Christmas party, and establishing how many girls and how many boys.

Having got all the information, the next step was to go to Norwich on a shopping spree. It was not possible to do the shopping in a single day, so we did it in a leisurely fashion. The Padre and his wife were responsible for half the purchases and my wife and I arranged to get the other half.

I may say we enjoyed our part immensely and we knew that the children would be delighted with their dolls or crayons or whatever we thought suitable.

I remember that particular Christmas, 1938. His Lordship spent it in Monte Carlo and so the staff were all free to enjoy the festivities. I remember clearly, I had bought a Father Christmas outfit and a large pair of white Wellington boots and was eventually ready and looking very much the part. At the appointed time I met the Padre and all his choirboys and, together with the village children, we formed a procession outside Stody Lodge and with myself and the Padre leading.

We headed for the village green of Hunworth and arranged ourselves around the great Christmas tree then ablaze with lights. There we were joined by the local inhabitants. A service was then held with the choirboys holding aloft their lanterns which they all carried. We sang carols with great gusto, everyone joining in the spirit of Christmastide.

The following day we arranged the party in the village hall for the children, the presents all having been suitably wrapped and hung upon the tree, and the trestle tables arranged and laden with goodies, with staff to spare to see that all went well.

The Padre and his good lady were present and I was masquerading as Father Christmas and at the appropriate time the presents were taken from the tree and handed to the children by me as their names were called. Excitement prevailed as the Padre and his wife removed the presents and passed them to me to distribute.

Happy laughter was all round and I overheard one youngster speculate, "That's not the real Father Christmas you know."

I know that each and everyone present had a very happy time thanks to their patron, Viscount Rothermere.

The same Christmas I received the following from Stratten House:

***Dear Chinnock,***
***Lord Rothermere sends this rabbit for your baby and hopes you all have a happy Christmas.***

*Yours sincerely,*
***H.Morison***

A few days later the Padre paid me a visit to talk of our success at Christmas and was delighted to hand me the following letter to read:

*VILLA ROC FLEURI*
*1 RUE DU TÉNAO*
*MONTE CARLO*
*January 12*

***My dear Padre,***
***Thanks for your letter. Lord Rothermere was delighted with news of the Christmas party. Chinnock is a very versatile young man and does his employer credit.***
***We have been having glorious weather here until a couple of days ago when rain fell, but even now, the temperature is delightful. I have felt sorry for all of you who have been freezing in Norfolk.***
***Best wishes to you and yours.***

*Very sincerely,*
***H.Morison***

Looking at the various correspondence that I have, I discover that I must have been quite busily engaged in diverse activities at that time, and I refer to the following letter:

*14*
*STRATTON HOUSE*
*PICCADILLY,*
*LONDON W.*

*December 12, 1938*

*Dear Chinnock,*
*His Lordship told me to write to you to confirm the authority he gave you to arrange an entertainment for the gardeners, gamekeepers, their wives and children and domestic staff.*
*When you have fixed the date will you, if necessary, see Mr Goude so that all the people under his control are free for the occasion.*

*Yours sincerely*
*H.Morison*

I had asked His Lordship's permission to use his dining room as a ballroom when we had met in London. "Use the house as you wish, Chinnock." he replied. I was a little worried, no, concerned I think is the word, as the dining room was lined with pale honeysuckle bark with a plain oak surround which would be an obvious place for a careless cigarette smoker to take advantage of. I therefore took special note of possible disasters and decided to get the footmen to clear the dining room completely, and also removed the furnishings to the drawing room which was then locked for safety's sake. We then had ample room at our disposal – we had the staff hall, the pantry and other staff apartments to accommodate the guests that arrived later. I had catered for 50 and wondered how to procure some music for the event. I eventually approached a local band from Holt and asked if they could help. They agreed to play from eight until eleven for £3 for a five-piece band; they called themselves the *Holt Owls*.

The evening's festivities were a complete success. Everyone was happy and there were no instances of anyone having too much to drink although there was ample of everything. I had addressed the company at the outset and had asked them to please be aware of the parquet floors, and had pointed out the care that should prevail in the dining room regarding cigarettes; needless to say, there were ample ashtrays available.

Some of the older people present preferred to play solo, whist or bridge and I allocated the pantry for that purpose. A running buffet was prepared in the kitchen and ran the whole evening. Eleven o'clock came and went and the band played on, they were enjoying themselves and also enjoying being refreshed at regular intervals. The local police had been represented, as was their wont. I had mentioned to the police sergeant that we were giving a staff party, so during the evening one or two of them looked in.

At 12.30, I announced that the party must end. During the evening spot prizes had been won by everyone, purposely bought and unobtrusively given, and as we bade our guests goodbye they were each presented with a ten shilling parcel of groceries which of course, at that time, was quite considerable. Whilst the staff were saying their good-byes, I returned to the *Holt Owls* leader who was holding forth on what a wonderful party it had been and that they would be only too delighted to be asked again. I reminded them that they had wanted to book only until 11 o'clock, but they said they had enjoyed themselves so much and in any case they were not called the *Holt Owls* for nothing. So they too departed full of praise for the entertainment.

Christmas was an exciting time, the Salvation Army would come with carols galore, and later on the Congregational Church choir and local choristers in small and large parties all received donations on behalf of His Lordship. The newspaper boys received their Christmas boxes which I paid out of my expense account as on this occasion the household staff – fourteen at that time – were in residence.

Being a country boy myself, I loved every bit of the estate. The woods were full of sweet chestnuts and pheasants, snipe and curlew lived on the more marshy parts of the countryside. A real paradise for bird life. We had over 100 nesting boxes arranged round about the pleasure gardens and I kept them all under observation and became quite familiar with their occupiers. There were green woodpeckers, both great spotted and lesser spotted also nuthatches and a host of tits of various kinds. We were even able, by making large enough apertures in some of the boxes, to encourage the little owls to nest and I spent many happy hours alone and sometimes in the company of Leonard Green – my second footman – but of course this was a springtime activity.

Shooting and fishing took up a lot of our leisure time. We had a small trout stream running through the estate that His Lordship had had stocked with fine salmon trout. He had given me his permission to fish, so I treated myself to a grand fishing rod. It might just as well have been my very own trout stream, because for the two seasons that I fished, I saw nobody else take advantage of it, I seemed to be the only person to own a fishing rod in the vicinity.

The winter of 1938 had left the trout stream in need of a spring clean, so the estate manager had given his men instructions to this end. Unfortunately, the people concerned in this operation were unaware of the fact that a metal mesh contraption, befouled with so much driftwood, when lifted would release a lot of our fish. Fortunately, the fish were en route to the mill pool which was still on the estate, so I was able to retrieve some of them at my leisure.

I had some grand times and experienced fishing round the clock, in stormy weather and in fine. Three- and four-pounders were frequently caught and, having really enjoyed myself, I would make my way homewards distributing my catch amongst the villagers of Hunworth who were always delighted to accept. Neither my wife nor myself were particularly partial to trout so the villagers and the staff at the Lodge came in for frequent treats, as also did the Padre and his wife. I was extremely fond of the art of angling in any form.

However, the shooting season in Norfolk and the golden October days I will always remember. For in November there was a great influx of bird life. Buzzards and other birds of prey soared aloft in circles whilst, at the same time, I often could spot a peregrine falcon and frequently a kestrel or a merlin. Short-eared owls in flocks of fifteen at times I saw and the gamekeepers on their early rounds found that long before they were up there had been an early arrival of jays and sparrowhawks. Around about this time, the fieldfare and redwing appcar and the number of song thrushes and blackbirds in the turnip fields was often perfectly amazing.

Colonel Wilfred Wild would bring a shooting party to Stody and they would be catered for in the traditional manner of guests of Viscount Rothermere. On their arrival the house would be decked with flowers and only the best would be the order of the day, as I would be wanting an excellent report regarding the service received during their ten or twelve days' shooting party.

I knew that our accommodation at the Lodge would not be sufficient but when Colonel Wild and his party arrived he would himself allocate his principle guests the quarters available and the overflow would be accommodated at the Guest House which was situated at the home farm a short distance away. There would be about ten or twelve guns in the party looking forward to an enjoyable stay, the only thing we could do nothing about being the weather, all other requirements were under control.

Colonel Wilfred Wild was a very nice person and most charming, as were the rest of his party and the staff and myself were keen to make a success and to see that they all had a most enjoyable stay with us. The shoot was already catered for; the head gamekeeper having decided which section of the estate should be used for the first and following days. The beaters, who would number about thirty, were all in readiness for the off and, of course, the dogs were trained especially to retrieve the game under the control of the keepers. So everything was ready for the next morning.

I had already received a fresh consignment of 12 bore cartridges from our supplier in Norwich to keep in reserve. However, our first concern was the dinner party on the evening of arrival. I had already gone through the menu with the kitchen staff and had come to an agreeable choice. We usually served five or seven course dinners and unless the host or hostess had any particular dish that they might ask for, everything was left entirely to the staff to compile the menu. The butcher's meat was all home killed and the finest sirloins, sweetbreads, pork, lamb – in fact just mention it to our family butcher, Turner, and it would be delivered. Lord Rothermere was very fond of lamb's tail pie, so when there was a surplus of these delectable tit bits available we were always pleased to take them as was also the case with fresh oxtails and 'only the best was good enough' was a local password as far as our catering staff was concerned.

Back to our guests and their dinner party. Everything went off well with two footmen and a parlour maid and myself in the dining room. As a course drew near to an end and the footmen were getting prepared to clear, I, who had stationed myself with a bell push at my back, would, at the appropriate moment, press it to alert the kitchen staff that the next course was then required to be ready, and so an orderly and steady flow of operations went off unhindered.

There was always sherry, red and white wine or hocks and champagne, Pol Roger or Krugs best vintages. Also a very popular and often called for was Château d'Yquem, a nice wine liked by the ladies. And so, the meal would progress until it was time for the dessert, at which time the table would be completely cleared, one footman carrying the butler's tray whilst the other stacked, removing everything including the lace dinner mats and used glasses. After this little ceremony, the dessert was served on beautiful Coalport dessert plates with finger bowls. The various fruits being handed round the table and then the residue placed on these perfect dessert dishes down the centre of the table. There were also nuts when in season.

After this operation, the two footmen who had served the coffee and put port wine and liqueur glasses on the table, took their leave of the dining room, as also did the parlourmaid who had assisted the clearing of the table. All three would soon be assisting the pantry boy in washing up the silver and the rest of the utensils that had been used.

In the meantime, I was the only servant alone in the dining room and I performed the rituals of serving the port wine or liqueurs and handing round the Corona cigars and cigarettes, Virginian or Turkish, and lighting the occasional cigarette for a lady or gentleman. After the handing round of the cigars and cigarettes they would then be replaced on the sideboard and at that time I could myself discretely disappear and leave the party to themselves, but knowing that within a few inches of the host's foot was a bell push under the carpet which would summon one of the staff at once. Usually the ladies left the gentlemen and retired to the drawing room.

Colonel Wilfred Wild always enjoyed his shooting, especially if he chose to shoot for partridge. I remember a certain gentleman in his party who, one could almost guarantee, would, when a covey of partridge was put up, take the leader of the covey with his right barrel and the last one with his left That is good shooting by any standard because when a covey of partridge take off they are in a hurry and fly very fast indeed.

I was very fortunate as the Colonel would invite me for a day's shooting and I looked forward to the occasion and we chose the day when the shoot was furthest from the house, which would make it a little inconvenient to be back by lunchtime. So we would have a picnic lunch arranged if the weather permitted and the footmen would meet us at a prearranged site with all the necessary refreshments. In the meantime I would be up with the guns as the beaters put the game up thoroughly enjoying the exercise and banging away. There would be frequent calls from the beaters of "cock up!" It was a most enjoyable day for me to be treated as a guest and partake of the party's pleasure, then at the appropriate time and place stop for a lovely picnic luncheon. What it was that made the food and drink taste so different in the setting of the Norfolk countryside, I never could resolve.

After about an hour or so and having enjoyed our meal, we then organised ourselves for the continuation of the shoot and when the keeper gave the all clear and the beaters had stationed themselves, we could continue. In the meantime, the footmen were clearing away the remains of our luncheon and packing the hampers into our old Austin staff car, to return to the lodge to get everything sorted out before the shooting party would be returning. Our shoot was a great success.

The head gamekeeper was pleased and the afternoon's sport was most enjoyable. There is not a nicer tasting pheasant than a Norfolk one; I always thought this, and I still do.

The keepers were very good at their jobs. Quite a lot of pheasants were hatched off each season, the breeding site being quite close to the gamekeeper's house, where rows of chicken coops were, at the appropriate time of year, occupied by broody hens on sittings of about 14 eggs per coop and when the pheasant chicks were hatched it was a delightful sight to behold. These chicks were watched over carefully and when big enough were freed to join their wild kind in the woods and clean straw and litter were laid in several clearance areas where food was distributed daily by the keepers until such time as they could fend for themselves. Fine wire mesh surrounded the shooting areas to keep them as confined and safe as possible. It can therefore be understood that with such good husbandry our shooting parties were ensured of being successful.

The vermin were relentlessly dispatched. Jays, sparrowhawks and other bird robbers, weasels and stoats were shot on sight and the keepers impaled their grim trophies upon the thorn bushes or barbed wire, not unlike the butcher bird or shrike will treat its victims and frequently one could come across such a grizzly sight in shooting country. Our head gamekeeper was a Mr Sturman, who was very good at his job. 250 brace of pheasant, often the result of a day's shoot, were designated for the game larder (of some considerable size), not to mention the rabbits, hares and sometimes also a few snipe.

To be able to write about my experiences makes my life more beautiful, as it intensifies and transfigures all the events and incidents that happened to me when I was a young man and fills me with inward happiness. I can recapture the feelings of walking in the pinewood paths with the sound of nature all around. These should not really have been my thoughts at the time, because with my .22 Remington Repeater rifle snugly tucked under my arm I was on the rampage for the odd rabbit, hare or pigeon. This put me in the position of a Dr Jekyll and Mr Hyde character, to be so in love with nature and yet prepared to shoot a defenceless creature.

It was interesting to note that whenever I carried a gun or a firearm, the wood pigeons, especially, were very alert and flew away in a flash but on other occasions, when unarmed, and taking a casual walk, they would stay to inspect my passing. I decided therefore to carry out an experiment and occasionally took a walking stick instead, which I carried under my arm, as I would my rifle, but they knew the difference, though how they did still remains a mystery to me.

As mentioned at an earlier stage in my book, I did quite a lot of rifle shooting and consequently became a very good shot and I will now relate how I came to be the owner of my Remington Repeater rifle.

Mr Harry Morison, Viscount Rothermere's financial secretary, originally brought the rifle to Stody Lodge and on his departure, he left it in my care and invited me to use it when I wished. I was delighted, and in due course took full advantage of my opportunities. He realised, of course, that I was familiar with guns and had been instructed in their usage; the safety catch always being on when the gun was loaded and the maximum care being taken at all times. A firearm should never be pointed at anyone and when rough shooting, one must always ensure that the gun barrel is first through a hedge. In the case of rifles, these can be dangerous in some circumstances, at one mile. It was nice, therefore, to have a very large estate at one's disposal.

On one occasion I was using the rifle in an area adjacent to the highway and decided to cross the road to another part of the estate when, on looking down the avenue, I could see a constable in the distance cycling towards me. I believe I have already stated that I knew all the local police and often talked with the sergeant over the 'phone, because of course, security was most important as there were many valuables at Stody Lodge and the police often called to see us and to check that everything was alright. On seeing the policeman bearing down on me, therefore, I thought it was P.C.Chapman and that I would wait and have a word with him. As he approached, however, I realised that it wasn't P.C.Chapman and in fact, when he got close, I knew for certain that I had never seen this officer before. The following conversation ensued: "Good morning Sir."

"Good morning Constable."

"Who do I have the pleasure of addressing?"

"Oh, I'm Viscount Rothermere's butler. I live in Stody Lodge, the house around the corner."

"And do you have permission to be in these woods?"

"Oh yes."

"And where is Stody Lodge?"

"Only five minute's walk away."

"You have a gun licence I presume."

"Yes."

"Very good sir, I shall be calling to see it as I shall be passing by again early this afternoon."

He then took his leave and I thought that would be the last I should hear of the episode. But no, I was with my wife when one of the footmen 'phoned to say there was a police constable to see me.

Off I went to Stody Lodge and again met P.C.Green (for that was his name). I asked him to follow me into the pantry where we would be alone. I then asked if he would like something to drink, but he said he didn't drink either and that he had just come to see my gun licence. Not possessing one, I said I didn't think I needed a gun licence for a rifle. He seemed surprised to hear that it was a rifle that I had been carrying. I asked him to wait a second while I went to the gun cupboard for the firearms certificate, and on reading it, he said it was perfectly in order except that it was made out for a Mr W.H.Morison, which wasn't my name.

By now I was regretting taking the rifle onto the highway as I realised I was at fault. The constable then asked if I had permission to use the firearm and I said I had used it with Mr Morison's knowledge, whereupon he said that he must get in touch with Mr Morison and where was he. I said he was abroad with Viscount Rothermere, and he asked where. I realised I was getting deeper into trouble and I said he couldn't get in touch with Mr Morison, that it was unthinkable, but he said he could. So in desperation, I said I was changing my story.

I had taken the rifle from the shooting cupboard and used it without permission. He said that wasn't what I had told him previously but I pointed out that there were no witnesses and that he would have to make out his report accordingly.

He took his leave shortly afterwards and I lost no time in getting in touch with the police sergeant to acquaint him with the particulars mentioned above. The sergeant told me to leave it in his hands and I was content to do so.

A week later, I received a letter from the superintendent, a cautionary one, telling me of the folly of my ways and that I must pay a fine of ten shillings and send it to Norwich. Having had this brush with the law I didn't use the Remington again until, at a later date, at a house party at Stody Lodge, I met W.H.Morison who, by the way, always enjoyed an aperitif before his dinner i.e. gin and mixed vermouth. During a talk, I told him the story whereupon he said, "Well you know Chinnock, I use the rifle so very little that I'll make a present of it then you can have the firearms certificate transferred to your name and there can then be no reoccurrence of this trouble."

In due course, I arranged to see the superintendent of police and the Remington became my personal property and I was able to continue with my shooting.

It was a beautiful little rifle and I would often go out for an evening's rabbit round up. I usually put twenty rounds up the spout and told myself there was to be no missing and I sometimes came back with a rabbit for each round of ammo. For practice, I rigged up a temporary range in the woods with Champagne bottles that were arranged through the knotholes in the fencing, so that the neck of the bottle faced me, and my target was to shoot down the neck of the bottles and blow the bottoms out. I became very adept at this exercise. There was one other young man in the neighbourhood who also had a rifle and we met on occasions. His rifle had telescopic sights, with which I disagreed because it's almost impossible not to shoot what you aim at and I thought that my kind of shooting was the more desirable.

One fine morning I was walking in the countryside with Leonard Green, our second footman, when we had to traverse a very large ploughed field. A slightly raised bank crossed through the centre and we were only able to walk in single file. As we were walking, we were discussing the fine furrows that stretched out on both our right and left when I suddenly espied a hare away on our right. When the hare had wind of us it decided to make itself scarce and started to lope away. The hare was some distance from us but I raised my rifle and remarked to Leonard "Watch him put a spurt on." Meanwhile I was following the furrow with my sights, then I pressed the trigger. There was a slight depression in the field at about that point, so we watched expecting to see it in full flight, but to our amazement, we lost sight of it completely. "I've hit him Lenny." I shouted.

"You couldn't possibly have done" he replied. However, to find out we walked down the furrows and to our utter surprise, there lay the hare. It was such a fluke we could hardly believe our own eyes and we decided to pace the distance back. It was 210 good paces and therefore a most extraordinary shot, a feat, an exceptional exploit I shall never forget.

We spent so many days exploring the countryside, but I remember one occasion in the spring, when we were happily engaged on a cross-country walk and quite suddenly, we came upon a covey of baby partridges, tiny little fluffy balls, about a dozen of them, cheeping away, and obviously surprised by our appearance. We were both intent on watching their antics, when one of the parent birds arrived on the scene. She flew within yards of us, then collapsed into an apparently helpless state, flapping and falling about in distress, thus taking over our interest. We both took a few steps towards the distressed creature, when to our amazement she took off like a bolt from the blue and when we turned again to look for the chicks, they too had completely disappeared. We had witnessed a parent creature's dexterity and intellectual adroitness in drawing the threat to her chicks, to herself, and in the meantime, presenting an object lesson to two interested humans. I shall relate more about my experiences of shooting later in this book, as I must describe the pigeon shoot with the tenant farmers and keepers, which was an annual event.

So back to Stody Lodge for the moment to try to describe some interesting details. Perhaps I may tell you of a typical breakfast that we might serve. Variety being the spice of life you may be sure we had it at Stody Lodge. Hot plates stood on marbled sideboards, on which would be placed silver dishes containing kidneys and bacon, eggs and sausages and kedgeree and kippers. Porridge was on the menu most breakfast times, as was haddock and poached eggs, all being kept hot and under constant observation. On an adjacent sideboard would be canapés of fruit; strawberries and raspberries tastefully arranged on Coalport stands that had been lined with grapevine leaves. Apples & pears, muscatel grapes, peaches & nectarines. Coalport dessert plates, silver dessert knives and forks. A beautiful sugar caster (Paul de Lamerie 1733) and several ornate cream jugs filled from our own dairy, freshly delivered that morning, it is not within my vocabulary to truly describe the silver in use in these houses but if I could ask the inventory keeper, Mr Herbert Cescinsky to do so, he would do it thus:

*"Set of four silver circular salt cellars 3 5/8 diam on four cabriole feet with cherub heads and swags above. Maker: Paul Crespin, London 1729, 44ozs 5DWTS (pennyweight), (Bateman-Hanbury Collection)"*

whilst my description would read: four lovely silver salt cellars, which is of course, what the layman would say. However, those four salt cellars are a priceless possession for its present-day owner whoever she or he might be.

There were, in some of the house parties, some very famous and renowned personages. Ladies would arrive with their maids and with most extravagant pieces of luggage in pigskin or crocodile skin, and with exquisite jewel cases which never left their sides. In fact, some ladies took charge of their own jewel cases. These cases were usually protected by outer covers with press-studs to prevent the actual leather coming into contact with the elements. Gowns were always most expertly packed with tissue paper ad lib. I know of these 'wrinkles' only through servant talk with the ladiesmaids themselves. Some of the gowns, it seemed, were beyond description and were a constant source of conversation amongst the female members of the staff. So much so, in fact, that on quite a few evenings, when there were fashionable ladies dining at Stody Lodge, I would be prevailed upon to leave a chink in the dining room curtains to ensure a peep by the domestic staff. We even had a rehearsal to make sure that the 'view' would be all that was required to give them food for thought, and this would be the topic of conversation for a while. But what corsages, what sheer line – and we were left in no doubt at all by the ladiesmaids as to how the end product was arrived at.

I remember one ladiesmaid who, while we were in Scotland, came into the housekeeper's room with a dress over her arm that must have cost £300 if it cost a penny. She laid it on the table to contemplate it.

"What are you going to do with that?" I enquired.

"It needs a little alteration." she said, reaching for a cigarette, and after a couple of puffs she put the cigarette down on an ashtray and took up a pair of scissors, snicked the bottom of the dress and then with both hands split it from the bottom to the top, in such a manner that I was heard to utter, "I hope you know what you are doing Kit."

"It's too bloody late now if I don't!" she rejoined with a laugh. This ladiesmaid was a Miss Kathleen Ponting, and a very accomplished needlewoman. She was the daughter of a tailoress of some repute. Incidentally, I met her again in 1978, whilst holidaying on the Norfolk Broads.

We certainly had some very elegant house parties in those days, and most enlightening conversation at the dinner table. I always admired the ease with which topics were discussed on absolutely any level. It really was a privilege to be able to listen to some very eminent personages holding forth, whether the subject was politics, general conversation or people and places. But back now to more mundane things that happened.

The household was wisely ruled and simply ordered, inasmuch that if any of the guests, at any time, expressed a wish to look at the servants' quarters or the kitchens, I was consulted as to when it would be most convenient, and I would accordingly instruct the staff to be on parade, as it were, and ready.

The staff quarters were separated from the rest of the house by a brass-studded baize door which could only be passed by appointment. Even Viscount Rothermere himself would enquire if it was convenient, when he decided he would like to inspect the wine cellar or staff hall.

He would often ask me what the staff were having for lunch, by way of a joke, and would follow up by saying he was sure the staff had better fare than he did. Manners were one of his priorities and I'm sure he inspired me to recognise that the happy way of doing things was by hospitality.

After all, my job was to see that all his guests were well looked after, and I always found it to be a glad duty as well as a delight. One day at Stody Lodge, His Lordship happened to be in the staff quarters when an open door caused a draught that blew some paper work onto the floor and he said, "What you need, my boy, is a paperweight and I've got just the thing for you, come with me." So I followed him into the hall where he picked up an ornament with a very heavy base and handing it to me he said, "There you are you can keep that on your desk, Chinnock, I'll make you a present of it." I thanked him and took it away. On closer inspection, I found it to be a presentation piece that had been sent to him from Hungary and it depicted the first aeroplane flight from Budapest to New York via Harbour Grace. It took the form of an eagle with outspread wings, perched on a globe of the world, with the route of the aeroplane clearly marked. The whole was worked in bronze and was standing on a marble base with an inscription plate written in Hungarian. It was, in fact, a very grand souvenir and which I am happy to say, I still have.

It was in the year 1939 when His Lordship presented me with a gift, that of an autographed picture of Adolf Hitler, in a lovely red frame. I regret, however, that I no longer have it as in the early war years I was advised by friends to get rid of it otherwise there could be repercussions. I may have been a suspect fifth columnist. Therefore, much against my own wishes, I did burn that picture, as it was quite possible for it to incriminate me if it was found in my possession.

So many things seemed to happen in my last year at Stody Lodge. One fine day the King's head gardener from Sandringham came to the gardens at Stody Lodge and spent quite a long time inspecting and commenting, and he seemed to be quite impressed and spent an enjoyable time with us. On taking his leave, he said to me that he would be only too delighted to show my wife and myself, or a party, over the gardens at Sandringham House at a convenient time. Unhappily, though, this never came to pass, as time swept us quickly forward into war, and I regretted not having had the pleasure of visiting the royal estate.

In the meantime, life continued most pleasantly. Mr Colin Brooks was installed in a fine old house on Edgefield, a couple of miles from Stody Lodge. Mr George Ward Price, foreign correspondent of the *Daily Mail*, had a house in Hunworth, and F.J.Clark, secretary, yet another house in Stody, and all contributed to the local atmosphere when they were in residence, which of course, was mostly when His Lordship was spending time at Stody.

My baby daughter was often the centre of attention. We had frequent calls from Mr and Mrs Colin Brooks, who would, from time to time, come and take afternoon tea in our cottage. Both were most interested in Hilary's progress and never missed a chance to pop in or maybe leave a teddy bear in the porch, or some other small gift, on special occasions. Also, Mrs Adelaide Wilson (Lord Rothermere's cousin) and her daughter, Miss Judith, would frequently ask if they could take charge of our daughter for a while. So she would be dressed in her prettiest frock and presented to the ladies, who often kept her for a couple of hours or so, either in the house or in the pleasure gardens where there was a most beautiful array of garden furniture. My daughter's favourite was a sun-lounger we called the *Ladybird* because of its hood which was covered with red spots on a white background. As I watched her antics in such wondrous surroundings, I felt myself wishing that she could have been more conscious, more aware of the whole scene, because so many lovely things were happiness for her. She was also in great demand among the staff, who would volunteer for baby-sitting, should the occasion arise. About this time, my wife was expecting our second daughter who was to be born at Stody.

I must tell a story now of a very dear old lady who kept a tiny general store on the Green at Hunworth; a little maiden lady named Miss Sewell. I remember the first time I entered her shop with the intention of purchasing a packet of cigarettes. A little bell which was attached to the other side of the door, clanged noisily and I was then confronted with this gentle looking old lady, dressed in a long black dress. “Good morning, Madam,” I said, “May I have a packet of 20 Players cigarettes please?” She was most profuse in her apologies, but she was afraid she had no packet of 20 cigarettes in the shop, but that she would be happy to oblige me with a packet of five, as she had no call for more than that normally. I asked if I might take four packets then, and she said of course I could. Having paid for my four thrupenny packets of five, I ventured to ask her if she would order some packets of twenty on her next order, and that I would buy them and become a regular customer. This was great news and she made no bones about it. She was so happy, in fact, that I confided to her who I was and that I was Viscount Rothermere’s butler and said I was sure he would be pleased to buy some cigarettes from her as well. I suggested, therefore, that she ordered me one hundred boxes as well, to supply the Lodge. I really made her day and she looked at me with a pair of happy old eyes. Her thanks were so warm that I might have just given her some fabulous gift.

I was to warm to this dear old lady, and so, besides purchasing hundreds of cigarettes from her, I put many other little pleasures her way, such as sending the car to pick her up so that she could walk around the gardens when it was convenient to both of us, and asking the head gardener to please pick a nice bunch of flowers that I could present her with on her leave-taking. Such happy memories, and that dear little lady was most delighted, and much more so when I mentioned that I had talked to His Lordship about her and that it was with his blessing that she should come to the gardens as often as she wishes. I’m sure she was greatly relieved, because I recall on her first visit, she appeared to be walking on forbidden ground.

I kept in touch with her for the duration of my stay in Norfolk and took her a trout once a week, when in season, or a pheasant on occasions, or maybe some strawberries or Cox’s apples from the fruit farm which, I must say, was a hive of activity at harvest time, with the sorting and packing of choice fruits.

Each Christmas was memorable for lots of Viscount Rothermere’s friends, and I wouldn’t like to suggest how many Norfolk turkeys, pheasants and Cox's orange pippins were dispatched each year, up and down the country, but the secretary always went to great lengths to see that nobody was overlooked, and each recipient had a choice Norfolk turkey in perfect condition and a nicely packed box of Cox's apples.

I had known the turkeys in their natural habitat and had watched their growth. Much care was bestowed upon their upbringing and they were often difficult to rear. All these things were of much interest to me and I never tired of being involved with nature.

Both my wife and I were delighted when, with the coming of winter, we were able to feed the pheasants which arrived outside our cottage each year asking to be fed. There were often great numbers, and they became so domesticated that we could pick them up at times, especially if we were in a wired-off corner. This happened when the snow was deep and made their natural foraging difficult. So they would come and we would feed them.

We also enjoyed our winter sports. The staff would decide where and when, and wrapped up in woollies and carrying large tin trays for sleighs, we would go to the nearest suitable site and commence to slide down the slopes, and after a while, but with much effort, we managed to get a nice runway which improved after each run as the snow became settled down.

I remember an incident which happened when I suggested to the head housemaid that if she would lie upon my back, thereby increasing the weight, we might go much further. No sooner said than done, we were off, increasing to a rather reckless speed and heading straight towards a thick hedge, and no way were we going to be able to stop our headlong dash into a very prickly situation. I yelled to my passenger to jettison herself, which she was very loath to do at speed, but with quite an effort on my part, I managed to tip her overboard, and continued on with my toes sticking frantically into the snow, endeavouring in this way to prevent going full tilt into the hedge. I managed to disengage myself from the makeshift vehicle, so as to meet the hedge broadside on, and I luckily achieved this with just a few minor scratches. In the meantime, the rest of the party came running to my rescue with yells of laughter at our undignified situation. Having picked ourselves up and de-iced our snow clogged wearing apparel, we decided to call it a day and made for our quarters as fast as possible, where a nice brew of hot soup soon put new life into us, and we were able to recap our experience afresh, and laugh about it all again.

I had a very good staff at that time. Eric Wakefield was first footman and, unhappily, was a war victim. Leonard Green was second footman and Stanley Walpole, who was to replace Leonard Green. I had been told to instruct him in the duties of a valet, so for a short period I had three footmen and a pantry boy, plus the cook and four female kitchen staff, and four housemaids. So when we had no residents, we represented quite a big family, and of course, the estate workers were ever present with seven gardeners for the pleasure gardens and kitchen gardens, and a Mr Tribe in charge of the glasshouses, and Mr Buckingham in charge of the home farms, the estate manager and the head gamekeeper plus three underkeepers. In fact, we were surrounded and felt far from remote. We were, in fact, more like a fortress, and all coming under the good husbandry of the local police, and at the same time, the staff were able, at any time, to take advantage of the staff car, an Austin 16 which was used for any emergency and frequently took the domestics to the local dances in the village halls.

I, at this time, had a car of my own, an Austin 10 saloon, with sliding roof, which I used on my frequent trips to Norwich. There were also two young chauffeurs, locally recruited. Each drove a Pontiac and they were stationed at the garage when not on duty further afield. I believe I have mentioned the head chauffeur, a Mr Bob Tanner who drove the Rolls 50 and who was almost constantly with His Lordship. There was also a Joe Higgs who drove a Rolls 25 and who was mostly in attendance on Mrs Adelaide Wilson and her daughter, Judith, and yet another Rolls 25 driven by a Mr Morton who frequently worked on the Continent, and incidentally, spoke French fluently. There was, therefore, always some interesting news whenever the staff could meet together, and it was on such occasions that we made the most of the current topics of conversation that circulated around the staff 'grape vine'.

We were all kept very busy whilst we had residents and so, of course, it was not until they had all departed that we were able to collect the happenings of the past week or so and put them into perspective.

I remember one gentleman in a house party who had arrived for the weekend, and when the time for his departure drew near, he approached me and went to the trouble of telling me that he was not used to being entertained in such surroundings and asked if I would be kind enough to tell him the amount of the tip that he would be expected to leave and to which of the staff he should leave it. I assured him that as a guest of Lord Rothermere, he was under no obligation at all and that he should feel free to do exactly as he liked in this respect. He thanked me, and as he said how well he had been looked after, I mentioned that five shillings on his dressing table would be an ample reward, and he could forget the rest of the staff. I believed this would put his mind at rest. He had been a most welcome guest, as were all the visitors to His Lordship's houses.

While I am on the subject of gratuities, I would like to approach tipping from another angle. The lady I choose to mention was Mrs Anthony Rothschild. Her method of showing her appreciation was as follows. On the morning of her departure, she would call me to her presence and say, "Chinnock, would you be so kind as to bring me a list of the household staff's names."

In due course, after the list had been forthcoming she would say, "Thank you, Chinnock and will you kindly come back in fifteen minutes."

Upon my putting in an appearance again, she would hand me a little pile of tiny black tissue lined envelopes, each with the name of one of the staff.

"Will you please deliver these for me?"

"Yes, of course, Madam."

"And then will you come back and see me yourself."

Having had the pleasure of delivering these greatly appreciated gifts to the footmen and to the rest of the household staff, I put in yet another appearance.

"Thank you for everything and this is for you." she would say. *This* was a ten-pound note. Thanking her, I would take my leave, the while thinking what a splendid way to be able to arrange things in so elegant a fashion. I was often surprised at some of the lovely presents I received from Lord Rothermere's guests.

All weekly wage cheques were paid to the wives of the married members of the staff because the staff being on the move so frequently, it was much more convenient for all concerned.

I recall a stay of six weeks in Scotland when, for most of that time, my wife was in London and, in between house parties, I was enabled to play some golf on the Royal Dornoch course, and also to do some shopping around for souvenirs for my family and friends.

I remember visiting a tweed maker, when I was able to watch the cloth in the process of manufacture. I had never seen a hand loom before and was intrigued and tempted to buy some, so I enquired the price of the cloth which I knew would make a magnificent plus-four's suit. I was told it was 30 shillings per yard and I agreed to take five yards. While the lady was serving me I was thinking how expensive it was, for at that time I imagine the average workman's wages would have been between 25 to 30 shillings, so I was being very extravagant, and, of course, I hadn't finished yet, because I had it dispatched, with my measurements, to Frazer's of Perth. I do remember, however, that I was more than pleased with the result.

The object of this report is to explain that having indulged myself and spent quite a lot of money on presents, I was still able to take back to London with me between 20 and 30 pounds pocket money, not having received any wages for that period, so it shows the lucrative nature of my gratuities.

To return to the staff at Stody Lodge, I had received the following letter:

*VILLA ROC FLEURI*
*1 RUE DU TÉNAO*
*MONTE CARLO*

***15th Jan. 1939***

***Dear Chinnock,***
***His Lordship seems to think Green is coming along very well and he wants you to train another young fellow for Stody, so that***

***Green can be used as a valet if circumstances require it.***

***Yours sincerely***

***H.Morison***

On the strength of this letter, therefore, I had engaged Stanley Walpole, who came to me on the recommendation of Lady Dashwood. He was to remain with us until the outbreak of war, by which time he had married one of the housemaids. His weekly wage was 30 shillings and he was also supplied with one undress livery, one morning suit, three white shirts and six white collars. These were considered to be very good perks at that time.

There was an excellent tailor who lived in Holt and he supplied our footmen and my own needs. We had the Gresham School in Holt to thank for his availability I am sure, as he also tended to all their requirements. In any event, he was a very good tailor and looked after us most professionally. He was a gentleman of the old school of tailors and his name, I remember, was Mr Knowles. Nothing seemed to be too much trouble, so our footmen were always very well turned out as a result.

Life at Stody was very good, but there was never a dull moment; anything could happen. I recall Viscount Rothermere arriving at Stody for lunch. This particular exercise happened on several occasions. He would arrive at the front door then make a beeline for the garden which was across the hall and through the drawing room, and out on to the terrace. He might then say, "What a lovely day, Chinnock! I think it would be nice to have our luncheon outside today."

"Very good, My Lord." I would reply.

He then took a leisurely walk, together with some of the guests whilst I, in haste, informed the footmen of His Lordship's wishes. Whereupon, there would be much activity, getting the garden furniture out of the summer houses, setting up the tables and arranging the chairs and then transferring all the silverware from the dining room including table napkins, linen etc.

By the time the party, which accompanied His Lordship, returned from their walk, we would be standing by, looking very pleased with our table which was laid and looking very inviting.

We would be congratulating ourselves on the speedy transfer, when His Lordship, who by this time had the biggest dahlia he could find in his buttonhole, would announce, "It's blowing up a bit Chinnock, I've changed my mind, we will eat in the dining room." Upon this 'as you were' and within ten minutes, order was restored and the luncheon would be served in the dining room. This often caused some amusement amongst the guests as well as, to a lesser degree, the staff.

There were times when we had started to serve a luncheon outside only to be caught in an unexpected sharp shower, and at such times utmost urgency prevailed, whilst we frantically salvaged all we were able to and started from scratch again in the dining room. All this was taken in great good humour by His Lordship, so the guests could hardly complain. On the contrary, they often would appreciate the situation, and appreciation is a great test of character.

I was privileged to meet very many great characters, so much so that I shall always remember them. Mr W L Warden was the first editor of the *Daily Mail* during my time of service, and he was a very nice man to know. He was followed by Mr Stanley Bell, another charming man indeed, and both these gentlemen had me on their list for complimentary tickets for the *Daily Mail* Ideal Home Exhibition. These would arrive in good time, and there were often more tickets than I could dispense with among my personal friends. It as a very pleasant privilege and one I appreciated. Mr A S Fuller of the *Daily Mirror* was also a very regular visitor at His Lordship's various establishments. All were gentlemen first, and certainly all of them were newspapermen to their fingertips.

I believe that at this time, Viscount Rothermere controlled the *Daily Mail*, *Daily Mirror*, the *London Evening News*, the *Sunday Dispatch* and the *Sunday Pictorial*, plus the *Continental Daily Mail* and the North of England publications of the *Mail*, and, I believe, other publications. I was sure, therefore, to meet many interesting people in the natural course of my activities in His Lordship's houses. Many I remember, but so also must there be many I have forgotten.

It was, however, the country life that I revelled in, and I would always be pleased if I got a call from one of the tenant farmers to inform me that they would be cutting a particular wheat field and inviting me to participate in the shooting that was available on such occasions. Being delighted, I would transport myself, with maybe another member of the staff, with our twelve bores and the necessary cartridges and arrive at the aforementioned field where the cutting was already in progress.

Having greeted everyone, we arranged ourselves about six or more guns around the field, at the ready to await anything, hare, rabbit, rat or vermin of any kind. Of course this exercise took time to develop and one could expect the odd shot in the early stages, but it got more interesting as the cover got less and less, and the odd rabbit or hare would make a dash for freedom, or rats that would be picked off as their short legs had trouble negotiating the three or four inch stubble. We often got a stoat or a weasel until the cover got so small that there was nothing to do but make a bid for it and that's when all the twelve bores were popping away and reloading as quickly as possible.

Then, just as suddenly, it stopped as the cutting of the field of wheat was completed and all the tally would be taken by the farmer, and the catch distributed. Then the dogs, who had been sharing the excitement, would come and make their presence felt and come in for a bit of a thank you pat for their share of the sport we had enjoyed.

We would then ascertain the following day's cutting of the harvest and make arrangements for meeting again for a repeat performance. These were happy days indeed.

One other annual event that I looked forward to was the pigeon shoot with the tenant farmers taking part. This would involve a drink or two at the local pub and a talk of proceedings to come. There were usually around twenty to thirty guns, including the gamekeepers, and each gun would be allocated a certain area of the home wood which was quite a large expanse. Later on in the afternoon, each one would take up his particular position to await developments, until such time as the birds would be coming in to roost, then gunfire could be heard from various quarters of the woods as time went on. Then there seemed to be much more urgency, and the shots were more frequent as the birds endeavoured to come in. They were coming into my section, so I was banging away at a flock which were heading into the trees. I got a couple and the remainder flew off again only to circle and try to gain entry to another part of the wood where other guns were waiting.

This continued, and the sound of the gunfire gave one the general position of the birds as they tried again and again to gain entry. This was most surprising, for these otherwise very intelligent creatures would persist in making repeated attempts to break through the ring of guns to get into their roosting positions in their home wood.

Each gun would account for about fifteen to twenty birds, and the day's bag could be around three to four hundred, for which the farmers would be pleased, as they are ravagers of crops to a degree not realised by the layman.

I will now take my reader back to Stody Lodge with its blue glazed tiled roof that shimmered in the sun all summer and still managed to sparkle in the depths of winter, when the snow lay deep and even. Due to our heating system, the roof remained free of snow or ice and always looked beautiful and in winter-time, in the still and quiet, the garden and woodland surroundings were indeed a veritable fairyland, and at such times I was pleased to be able to study the footprints of the various creatures who lived in our vicinity.

**AT THIS POINT**, and in this year as we approach the world upheaval, I would like to recapture some of the situations I experienced with Viscount Rothermere, and recall a series of situations which I will call anecdotes, and these I recall with pleasure.

His Lordship was on his way to Stratton House in the company of one of his secretaries and had a bunch of violets thrust towards him by a flower seller, which he accepted and gave the good lady a one pound note, and refused to take any change. Upon which, the cockney lady was so profuse with her thanks and her "God bless you Sir!" that he gave her another pound note and left her quite jubilant.

Surely one of her most fortunate days! Arriving at the flat ahead of his secretary, who was delayed in the hall with some correspondence, he was received by my wife who opened the door. "Here you are, my dear." said His Lordship, "A little posy for you." and then proceeded to his desk in the sitting room. Shortly afterwards, upon the arrival of F.J.Clark, the secretary, I was in his office when he asked what the old man did with the bunch of violets he bought in the morning. "He gave them to my wife." I answered, to which he replied, "I doubt whether your wife will ever receive a more expensive bunch of violets." It was then that I learned that he had paid two pounds for a commodity which was on the market for sixpence, at that time. Lord Rothermere was delighted to do such things.

On other occasions, whilst in the lift on his way up he would ask the lift-boy a question, maybe on current news – anyway something topical, and if he got a bright answer, the lift boy would get a big tip.

One day His Lordship was dining alone at the Flat, a very rare occasion, and he said to my wife who was serving him a meal, "Are your people well, my dear?"

"Yes, thank you." she answered.

"And has your father plenty of work?"

"No My Lord, my father is unemployed at the moment."

To which he almost yelled, "What! And I own a paper mill close to your home."

He called Clark, his secretary, who was on hand and told him to see that Rose's father was permanently employed at his factory, and to give Rose £25 and two bottles of champagne to take to her mother and father. He then said that she should have told him before as he could have saved her parents needless worry. My wife's father was employed at Reeds Paper Mills and worked there for 20 years until his retirement, and was paid a pension until he died in 1979 at the age of 97.

A very amusing situation developed one afternoon at the Flat in Stratten House, when a certain lady who shall remain nameless, remarked to His Lordship, "You know Harold you pay your staff exorbitant wages, no one in London pays as much as you do."

"Oh, do you think so, my dear?"

"Clark, bring me a list of staff wages."

On being duly presented with a list the lady looked over His Lordship's shoulder and said, "Yes, look! Who else pays their chauffeurs £15 per week – it's much too much."

"Well, Clark," said His Lordship, "we had better do something about this, so will you double the staff's wages."

This was His Lordship's idea of a grand joke, and it was quite a few weeks later that he remembered and asked Clark if he was still paying double wages. "Yes, My Lord."

"Well you had better revert to normal, I think, otherwise I'll be going broke."

Another amusing story I have to tell took place in Norfolk. His Lordship was on his way to Stody when, just outside Norwich, where his son The Hon Esmond Harmsworth owned quite a large estate; he saw a group of young boys with bunches of lily of the valley, picked from the nearby wood. He told the chauffeur to stop the car and was then offered these sweet smelling nosegays. He took a couple of bunches and paid the boys some money then remarked, "Wherever did you get these flowers from my lads?"

"That big wood over there Sir, it belongs to a millionaire and he'll never miss them."

"I don't think he will either." said His Lordship with a meaningful look at Tanner, his chauffeur as they drove on their way once more. Incidentally, lily of the valley was one of Lord Rothermere's favourite flowers and the story is typical of the man, a man as rare as a butterfly in a snowstorm.

I recall another incident. My wife had had the great misfortune to drop and smash a loving cup, costing several hundred pounds, at Stratten House and was beside herself with worry and anxiety awaiting His Lordship's arrival, and could hardly wait to blurt out "Oh My Lord, I've had a terrible accident, I've broken your loving cup."

"Bring me a cup of tea my dear." he said as he walked towards his sitting room. The cup of tea was forthcoming, but with more tea in the saucer than anywhere else. "Put it down, my dear and tell me what happened and please, don't be so upset." After listening to her story he said "Look here, my dear you mustn't cry over broken glass or broken china – broken arms or broken legs, yes, they are precious and anyway if I thought I could make you feel better you could break that Ming vase over there. The loving cup I remember was a beautifully engraved specimen especially made for the accession to the throne of King Edward VIII. These experiences live with one forever.

In a lighter vein, I wish I could put my reader in a similar set of circumstances. For instance, have you ever felt you were the centre of attention? This was the picture, often I would be in the sitting-room and Viscount Rothermere would say "Peal me a peach!" Now he would not be alone, he often had several people with him, and he didn't mean I could peal the peach unobserved, no, I must prepare the peach in full view, and if you have ever tried to peal a peach without handling it, you will appreciate the predicament I was in. For he was a great humourist and would relish the possibility of my dropping the peach during preparation.

These little episodes tend to enlighten the more human side of a great man. I remember instances that were typical, such as when he would take a walk in Hampstead and would go into the butcher's shop he knew in his youth and purchase a pound of sausages and on returning to his house would give instructions that he would like them for his breakfast. On other occasions when returning from Norfolk to London, he would have Tanner, his chauffeur drive via Yarmouth just so that he may procure a box of kippers, and on arrival at the Flat, he would say to me, "Here you are Chinnock, a box of Yarmouth Kippers, put some in your Frigidaire and send the rest to Avenue Road."

But above all, he was a great patriot, and had at this period published two books – *My Fight to Re-arm Britain* and *Warnings and Predictions*, and I was pleased to receive one copy of each (autographed copies).

He was the instigator of the *Britain First*, the aircraft, powered by two 645hp Bristol Mercury engines, which was built by the Bristol Aeroplane Company and, after trials, was presented to the Royal Air

Force in the name of the *Daily Mail.* The military type developed from the *Britain First* and was christened the Blenheim bomber. Of the Blenheim it was then reported that it was a mid-wing all metal, twin-engined monoplane, then in production. It was reputed to be the fastest bomber in the world, which indicated that her speed must have exceeded 300 mph, but the actual figure was a guarded secret. A model of the plane had an honoured place on His Lordship's desk and came under my special care. The fact that it was left to a civilian enthusiast to inspire and provide what was to prove a striking addition to our national defences must have made him feel very proud indeed. For me it was a most interesting period of history, I was a silent witness, privileged to be present at the unfolding of very stirring events.

ꕥ

**BUT TO RETURN TO STODY LODGE** in 1939; it was a very busy time, as on instructions from His Lordship, I was ordering alternative lighting for Stody. "You must be prepared, Chinnock." His Lordship had told me, "and if the electricity gets cut off we shall all be in the dark."

I had, therefore, bought a large selection of Tilley lamps. F.J.Clark's house at Stody had been an eye opener for me, as he had installed some very good lighting, his house not being on an electric supply and so with this know-how I got several sorts, some hanging and some standard lamps and a large supply of paraffin which I stored in the out-house and, as the year wore on, His Lordship, from time to time, asked me to store something or other in my cottage. "Roll up this carpet, Chinnock, it's very valuable." Although there were pictures worth a fortune and in the hall, we had some very valuable Canton enamel and up the oak staircase, the walls were hung with *Cries of London* pictures.

One day he said to me, "Chinnock, I want you to pack that Ming vase very carefully for me as it could shatter very easily, so will you see to it." So I had a wooden case made which was larger than the vase. I stuffed the vase with cotton wool and then stuffed the case with cotton wool and very carefully sealed the lid, and the next morning I got in touch with Mr Herbert Cescinsky to inform him of the inventory number of the Ming vase and what I had done. "Where have you put it?" he asked

"I have it in my cottage with several other things."

"For God's sake take care of it Chinnock, that vase is worth £3,000."

We had the house camouflaged around about this time and a local man from Holt made a very good job of it, so now our blue pantiles were khaki brown and black and after a couple of weeks the house had merged into the hues and colours of the woods they nestled in, and the only thing that still looked rather uniform was the swimming pool.

The house parties continued nevertheless and we endeavoured to keep the thoughts of war at a distance. We had more shooting parties and life continued to be very agreeable.

We had an outside larder which was quite large, and I had arranged with the kitchen staff to conserve as much as was possible. I had purchased dozens of Kilner jars for jam and chutney, and in a few months, we had a considerable store which, together with a goodly store of honey, was quite a sizeable cache for the future. His Lordship, when next on a visit was highly pleased with our efforts and said, "Well done my boy, and it might be a good idea to get as many candles as you can lay your hands on, they are always a good standby in an emergency." So when on a later date I happened to be in Norwich, I had a very amusing experience. My wife and I took a walk around Woolworth's store and stopped at the counter where candles were to be seen on display and having satisfied ourselves of the size that we would require, I asked the young lady assistant, who was waiting to know our requirements how many candles we could purchase. "As many as you please, Sir." she replied.

"Then we would like 500 if you could manage that amount." Her expression was a picture to behold. She looked at us in disbelief "Did you say 500, Sir?"

"Yes" I replied.

"I'll have to fetch the manager." she said and looked at us both suspiciously, as much as to say, "There are a couple missing from the loony bin." The manager arrived in due course and he also looked us over. Why do you want 500 candles if you please, and was there anything more we wanted? Yes, we may as well take 24 candlesticks. In the meantime, I had enlightened the manager that we were preparing for future emergencies and he eventually could see the funny side of the situation.

Writing of this episode at this date and time, it may interest my readers to know the cost, which I have just ascertained from my expense account: F.W.Woolworth's 500 candles £1.5s.0d. and 24 candlesticks 12s/7d. Even I, now, can hardly believe this ever happened, but it certainly did, though in another world, it seems.

Norwich is a city that we enjoyed greatly. The Cathedral and the surrounding area is steeped in history. There are two Norman chapels which date from 1096. The Castle was a Norman keep but is now a museum and we were always happy to be able to explore and find interesting facts of past history.

Having my own car at this time made it simpler to explore the surrounding countryside. We visited Walsingham, best known for its Priory ruins, dedicated to Our Lady of Walsingham. A popular shrine in the Middle Ages, it is on the River Stiffkey, five miles from Wells, and took me back to the famous, or should I say infamous stories of the Rector of Stiffkey and a certain Barbara Harris, which kept the newspapers fully occupied for some lengthy period, and 'made' the News of the World for highlights. The Rector, I believe, ended his life in a barrel at a side-show some years later. I am uncertain of the details, but I believe they involved a lion.

Another favourite place was Blakeney Point, a bird sanctuary covering some 1,100 acres, a veritable haven for the bird lover where could be seen goldeneye, smews, gooseanders, pintails, shovelers, tufted duck, pochards, widgeon, mallards, teal and coot, black headed gulls, Egyptian and Canada geese in numbers and moorhens in great quantities. Whilst on the marshes there might be seen, at a safe distance, great flocks of pink-footed geese, feeding at leisure. I was fortunate, in as much as I had the time to stand and stare. Today, of course, there are untold thousands of nature lovers and bird watchers who can be seen with their field glasses and cameras, but in my time one could observe almost alone, and would appear as an oddity rather than the general rule, and if one possessed a box camera, as indeed I did, taking pictures was much more difficult.

I remember, on one occasion at Stody, to enable me to get a picture of a great spotted woodpecker, I had first to put the camera on a bough of a tree at the desired distance, and fix it securely in place and then attach a piece of strong cotton to the shutter release, which was then threaded through a series of metal loops to a hide on the ground, where, when all was checked, I would sit in wait and hopefully I would get a picture. I carried out this exercise, when I knew there were young in the nest, which ensured that I would not have to wait so long for one of the parent birds to appear. When having one or other in the desired position I would pull the cotton which would release the shutter, the noise of which was sufficient to scare my feathered friend away again.

Woodpeckers especially, are very furtive birds, as are the nuthatches and I found them quite difficult to photograph, but at least I had several successful results, though not to be compared with today's advanced techniques. Sufficient to say, however, that it made a very happy pastime for me at that time.

I was also much interested in the woodcock and the snipe, the latter being a marsh frequenting, long beaked bird and owing to its darting flight, is a very difficult bird to shoot and makes popular sport for the expert, who aims at the 'zig' and shoots at the 'zag' as it were. The woodcock is very like the snipe and is also shot during the season and is regarded as a table luxury. Both these species being found quite plentifully in the county of Norfolk.

My wife, in the meantime, was happy with our baby daughter and our little Maltese terrier, Judy. Judy, if you remember, I mentioned had a brother who was called 'Punch' and lived at Avenue Road, Swiss Cottage with Miss Judith Wilson. Both Miss Wilson and her mother were frequent visitors to Stody Lodge, and on one of their visits they brought along Punch. Upon being introduced to his long lost sister, he was overjoyed and so it was that they met quite frequently from then onwards, and Miss Wilson and her mother seldom visited us without bringing Punch. During the summer months Punch and Judy could be seen romping together in the pleasure garden, to the delight of the onlookers which often included my daughter Hilary in the company of the ladies who always found time to entertain her and of course the opposite would be true as she would also be entertaining them.

But the dogs, Judy with a pink ribbon on her head and Punch with a blue one in his, were most amusing and posed a special charm in that beautiful setting, whether it was the massed yellow and blue crocuses beneath the mountain ash trees which grew on either side of the terrace, or by the swimming pool, or later on in the year, the rose gardens, in fact, just anywhere was special.

The springtime was most lovely. There were woodland paths that wandered off from the great lawn in great sweeps between the natural background of full grown firs and conifers, and so massed were the daffodils and narcissus of every kind imaginable and under one great fir tree a blanket of King Alfred daffodils with their great yellow trumpets standing almost eighteen inches high, a picture of magnificent splendour, the whole of which would have taken two men with scythes a day at least to cut them all.

We had spring flowers every day when required and never noticed the difference, for there was always a 'host of golden daffodils' as well as myriads of narcissus, standing shoulder to shoulder like silent and beautiful sentinels, wafting their perfume on the gentle breeze and to me, anyway, it was a heaven on earth. Why, we even had a eucalyptus tree in our heath garden and berberis of many kinds too numerous, even if I knew their names, to describe. The whole, being kept in first class condition by the gardeners who could always be seen busy and obviously enjoying their labours. The lilacs were very special with great pendulous clusters in purple, mauve and white, and their heady perfume would betray their presence when being approached.

When there were no residents, the staff were at liberty to enjoy the delights and to take walks about the estate, but on such occasions we often went further afield for our pleasure. We would make up a party for an evening's outing in Norwich, where we could choose a theatre or picture show, but more often than not, we went dancing at Samson and Hercules. My wife and myself, with a couple of footmen and the housekeeper and one other maid, made an admirable little party to dance the night away, and to partake of the refreshment that was at hand. The liquid refreshment that the ladies seemed to be most partial to were cocktails that were called Green Goddesses. We always had a thoroughly good time and before we knew it, it would be past midnight, and soon we were on our way home in boisterous and happy mood. Twenty miles of country roads before we would eventually arrive back at Stody and now, in the early hours, we would, if we felt hungry, and we often did, have a cook-up in the kitchen before retiring. Kidneys and bacon and sausage or anything that we would fancy and maybe some cold pheasant or some York ham. Yes! they were very happy times and we were very privileged to have enjoyed them.

While on the subject of food, I recall the ice cream produced at Stody was simply delicious, strawberry ice was, for instance, made from the choicest of fruit sent in from the fruit farm and which was then carefully passed through hair sieves until the desired amount was produced. This then, with sweetening agents, was mixed together with fresh pure cream from the dairy, the whole then put into a drum which stood upright inside the ice cream tub, the outside of the drum having been packed with broken ice and freezing salt. The handle would then be anchored into place, which when turned, made the drum containing the mixture spin around inside the ice-packed container and the more briskly it turned the sooner the desired result. The eating of this was a pure delight, so we would often have served for sweet, a concoction called the Ice Bomb. This would be served with spun sugar and could be strawberry, raspberry or vanilla ice. The spun sugar was obtained by melting sugar and colouring with various agents then quickly being whisked between two metal pokers protruding from the edge of the workbench. These were placed at about a distance of eighteen inches apart and producing a gossamer effect which could then be placed around the huge ice cream ball with the multi-coloured spun sugar; this was a sight to behold.

The catering, which was of the highest order, was always greatly assisted by the very high standard of materials to hand, as these were always of the very best, it really was difficult not to excel in our efforts. Presentation was also taken care of in the use of beautiful silverware enhanced by the suitable garnishings available.

I discovered one secret of life and that was how difficult it is to choose when 'the world is your oyster', and that I would much rather work for a millionaire than to be one. Between simple and noble persons, says a great philosopher, there is always a quick intelligence they recognise at sight, and this I believe to be true. So I never minded being in my particular position, the situation was an ideal one for me, and when it all ended it was very sad.

We were well into the year 1939 when I received another communication from Scotland:

***Dear Chinnock,***
***When Green gets back to Stody, His Lordship wants you to give him some instruction in the duties of a valet. He is a very pleasant young fellow and should get on well.***
***Yours sincerely***
***H.Morison***

In the meantime, I had received at Stody Lodge, general consignments of stores from Fortnum and Mason to be held in case of emergency. These to be checked and storage space to be found for them. So there was quite a lot of activity in that direction. Among our varied assortment of preserves were three tea chests of *Silver Teapot* tea, a delightful, if expensive, brand of tea which excelled *(sic) Earl Grey,* or so was the opinion of our household. That's as maybe, but undoubtedly they were two of the finest brands obtainable at that time.

I was also supplied with coffee, which was used in all our households, from a firm called Legrain, whose headquarters were in Soho, and whose products were most excellent. So much so, in fact, that I was often asked by some of the gentlemen where we bought such coffee, as it was simply out of this world, and I would answer, "Legrain's of Soho."

Lord Rothermere was also very fond of oysters supplied by Scoll's, the oyster people in Piccadilly, and would have as many as two dozen Scott's Imperials, in his oyster sauce, which would accompany an appropriate dish or course.

On the occasions when I went to any of our tradespeople, I was treated in the most grandiose fashion. It was, in fact, an experience to walk into a shop like Fortnum & Mason's where every male assistant was to be found dressed in immaculate morning dress, and would overawe all but the bravest heart. For me, at least, my journey was unnecessary, as a 'phone call would find them all bending over backwards to execute the slightest whim of my illustrious employer. Nevertheless, I would add, that to visit such a place was a delight to remember.

Recently, for instance, whilst I was in London, it was rather a nostalgic exercise to visit the store again, only to wish I hadn't, for nothing was the same. Of course, I couldn't afford to buy any of the goods on offer, they were completely out of my reach, but that had nothing to do with it, I did see a couple of assistants in morning dress, but the atmosphere I had once known, had completely disappeared; I can surely say it will never be there again. I hope this is a very interesting experience for the present generation to read about.

Leonard Green had returned once more to Stody Lodge, after a stay at Burghfield House, and was speculating on what was afoot, as I had acquainted him with the instructions which I had received regarding his valeting abilities. He was an apt pupil at cleaning and pressing and the laying out of dress clothes and other secrets of the valeting business, so I let events take their course and carried on with the routine working of Stody.

# Chapter XIV

# CHAMBERLAIN DECLARES WAR

**I HAD BY NOW ALREADY READ** Viscount Rothermere's book *Warnings and Predictions* which he had autographed for me at Easter.

So when, in September, we heard the declaration of the Rt Hon Neville Chamberlain that we were at war with Germany, after Hitler had invaded Poland, we were surprised of course, but not so surprised as the general public, I think – for had we not been expecting this world tragedy for the past two years? The staff and myself listened to the official declaration that was broadcast on the wireless, and wondered about our individual circumstances and what would be the outcome of it all.

I almost expected air raid sirens the next day or so and these would surely come later, but for the present it was business as usual. We had a house party soon afterwards which included, besides Mrs Adelaide Wilson and Miss Judith, Sir Max and Lady Pemberton, and His Lordship spent some time with us about this time.

Things were getting a bit panicky in London and evacuees were seeking ways to escape, so Viscount Rothermere said to me, "Chinnock, we must do something to help, and quickly. Can you organise the Guest House to receive some evacuees from the East End of London."

"Yes, My Lord," I replied.

"Get what you require from Norwich, beds, blankets, cots, prams or pushchairs, anything you need. The Padre will give you some help I know. Could you take say twenty or thirty women and children?"

"I'll do my best."

"Alright my boy, keep me informed."

After His Lordship had returned to London, therefore, we set about doing his bidding and after a great buying spree in Norwich and the transporting of the same, we had the Guest House almost ready, and on a day or so later came the evacuees. We took about twenty, that is children with their mothers, and we installed them in the accommodation we had prepared, and sorted out the prams, pushchairs, cots, beds and the bed linen, blankets etc.

They seemed to be so miserably unhappy and deeply depressed, with their children crying and suffering bodily discomfort, that refreshment of some sort was called for, and that was attended to as soon as was possible. They would cater for themselves once installed and settled down. They were a very sorry sight, and were all from the east London area. After explaining where the nearest shops were and how far away the public house was, we left them to sort themselves out. Milk from the farm, which was adjacent, would be supplied free but even from the first day, I think the countryside confounded them and there was an air of perplexity and they seemed overcome by the quietness of their surroundings. The children were mostly in arms but there were a few toddlers as well.

We left them to their own devices and returned to our duties at the Lodge, though not with our usual gusto, as the staff all seemed to be unsettled and were all wondering, no doubt, what might be the final outcome for each and everyone, and each well knowing that the Christmas festivities which lay ahead would be the last that we would all enjoy together.

So we resolved to make the most of our opportunities, we went on many happy outings to Norwich, and danced, and talked to people we met, only to realise that most people were making the most of their lives and having the last fling, as it were, and living in a 'cloud cuckoo land'. People were leaving their usual haunts. We would suddenly realise that a familiar face had disappeared and, on enquiry, found they had joined one of the services.

I hadn't passed my driving test at that time, so was speedily issued with a defence of the realm certificate that gave me full rights to drive any vehicle. These conditions brought home to me the realisation that we must all use time as a precious gift. I had also joined the ARP at about this time and was finding out all about poison gasses and the effects of such attacks, and fire fighting. Stirrup pumps and bomb disposal, and altogether getting a good briefing as to what lay ahead.

Sir Max and Lady Pemberton were with us for the Christmas festivities as also were Mrs Adelaide Wilson and her daughter Miss Judith. We had our usual Christmas trees festooned, and so we were ready and on the threshold of our last great jollification at Stody Lodge. Sir Max Pemberton had prevailed upon Mrs Adelaide Wilson to let his son, who was a young naval officer, be included as a house guest and, of course, he was readily accepted.

Soon to arrive, therefore, was this very young tall smart young man, lately commissioned in His Majesty's Navy and looking every inch a sailor in his brand new uniform. This was Sir Max Pemberton's son by his second wife. So Christmas was with us once more, the carol singers had been, that is, the local children. We also had the Church Army and the Salvation Army, all singing beautifully and most appreciated by our household and standing in a semi circle at our front door making a most seasonal scene.

The newsboys had been for their Christmas boxes, as also had the postgirls. I had the very pleasant duty of performing the distribution of largess on behalf of a very generous employer, and I kept an expense account for this purpose and no one went away empty handed.

Christmas was a happy time for all. Our Christmas fare was most sumptuous and a very experienced kitchen staff contributed to our success in the dining room, which, with its impeccable table linen and Brussels lace tablemats, left nothing to be desired. We had Christmas crackers from Fortnum & Masons, so how could we go wrong, but alas we did.

It was after dinner, and I was called into the drawing room where Mrs Wilson complained to me about the behaviour of young Mr Pemberton. I had served coffee, liqueurs, cigars and cigarettes and replaced the cigars and cigarettes in their silver box on the sideboard as usual, and I had taken my leave from the dining room. The footman, Green, had gone back to the dining room after a little while, to retrieve the coffee cona, when, as Mrs Wilson related the story to me, young Mr Pemberton shouted to Green, "Will you please get the cigarettes and put them on the table beside me and leave them there." She was very cross indeed and said that she would inform His Lordship of his bad behaviour and that he had been most rude. I mentioned that he was a young man who was soon to go to sea and that I was sure he had not meant to be rude and I hoped, as I took my leave, that the matter would go no further.

There was no shortage of cigarettes, they were kept in each room, and even in the front hall there could be found a silver box, ever available, so the incident didn't seem important to me, and I had forgotten it, when a few weeks later, His Lordship being in residence, called me aside one morning and said, "Chinnock I hear you had a bit of trouble with young Mr Pemberton at Christmas."

"Not really My Lord" I replied, "it was only that Mrs Wilson took exception to the incident."

"I know all about it, the ladies explained his behaviour, and Chinnock, I'll have you know that I will not tolerate my staff suffering any insults under my roof by any of my guests, and for your information that young man will never be a house guest here again."

It was an unhappy set of circumstances ever to have happened at all, for he had only been with us for a very short stay and was away on active service within a week or so and after a few weeks, tragedy struck on his first ship and he was killed in action. A smart young man, no more than a boy perhaps, but such were the fortunes of war. I had many more shocking experiences in front of me when I myself had to take an active part in open conflict between nations and see and witness atrocities beyond belief, but these were things to come. Nevertheless, I grieved with and for Sir Max and Lady Pemberton.

Viscount Rothermere asked me to accompany him to South Africa early in the year of 1940. I had mixed feelings about going as my wife was now pregnant, but no sooner had I explained the situation than he said, "Your place is with your wife Chinnock; I'll take Green with me."

I confess that I didn't relish the trip at all, especially under war conditions. Leonard Green, on the other hand, was keen to have such an opportunity put in his way, and after being kitted out at Austin Reed's was ready, and had left within a few days.

I, on finding the house party now consisted of the ladies Wilson and Sir Max and Lady Pemberton, settled down again to a routine of sorts, as we had been having some of our evacuees getting very dissatisfied with their lot and threatening to go back to London.

At the outbreak of war, Viscount Rothermere had insisted that none of the Rolls Royce cars would be used and would lay them all up for the duration and keep but one small Austin car for the use of Mrs and Miss Wilson. I had my own Austin 10 which I used to drive Sir Max & Lady Pemberton if they wished to go to Holt or to drop or pick them up at the station as they wished. They had gone back to Queen's Gate in London for a couple of weeks.

During that time, a couple of the staff and myself had gone down to the Guest House as two or three of our charges had gone back to London. We found that the conditions down there left a lot to be desired. They were living in squalor and all the nice new blankets which we supplied, and the rest of the bedding, were in a sorry state indeed. The head housemaid who was with us took the situation in hand and we had a very distasteful job on our hands, but we did improve matters a little. Some of the women and children had gone back to London and the remainder were thinking of doing likewise, and secretly we were hoping that they would, as we would be well rid of them.

A few days later, we were still of the same opinion, when three of us contracted impetigo, a disease of the skin. Our local doctor was quickly called and he confirmed our suspicions and left us with large bottles of Dettol and wads of cotton wool and instruction that we must be constant with our endeavours to get rid of our afflictions. Our daughter, Hilary, was unfortunate enough to have it affect her ears, which made it a difficult exercise for us and a painful one for her. We had the ladies in the house, so we did our best to isolate ourselves from them.

A day or so later the rest of our evacuees took to the road, taking prams and pushchairs and anything else they wanted. We were happy to see them go and we eventually had a bonfire and burnt the urine sodden mattresses and disinfected the quarters that they had occupied. It took a fortnight to rid ourselves of our unhappy state and, in the meantime, I had received a letter from Sir Max as follows: (dated 5th March 1940).

***Dear Chinnock,***

***I am much obliged for your letter and your thoughtful contribution of the butter and sugar – most welcome. I enclose a cheque for Robinson's bill with my thanks. Of course, I could not come to Stody while you have a sickness. If you get a clean bill of health at Easter, I should like to be with you then, and Lady Pemberton. We will let you know and trust you to let us know how things progress. So many thanks. Kindly give our best remembrances to the ladies, who I trust are well.***

***Yours most sincerely,***
***Max Pemberton.***

By now, rationing had come into being, and lots of other legislation, like petrol rationing. Luckily, we still had quite a lot in our tank at the garage, so for the present we were not affected.

Spring was just ahead and the spring flowers were well in advance and showed great promise. I was still able to go shooting and fishing, but when I did indulge, it seemed to me that I was trying to turn back the clock.

Everything had suddenly become so very temporary and lemming-like. It seemed to me that the world was rushing headlong into disaster hitherto unknown to man.

With the spring upon us, I was doing my favourite trips to visit the bird boxes and sharing the nesting activities of a great assortment of bird life.

Some boxes I found to be fouled, or needing other attention and I would remove old nesting material and leave them nice and fresh only to find a few days later that a lot more desirable residences were taken.

I took more than usual pains this springtime on my self-imposed duties towards my feathered friends because I knew that this would surely be the last time that I would have the privilege of doing so.

I took my time and savoured the sweet, pleasant odour and would remember the fragrance of the countryside, and no matter what lay ahead, I would live for the moment, the memory of which would be so ingrained, that it would be almost instantly recalled to mind, and so it seems it must have been, for now, more than forty years on, the memory is so keen that I can still remember minute details of the happy days I spent at Stody. I made it a special occasion to visit the gamekeepers and, as often as possible, to watch the progress of the young pheasants that were being hatched under cooped hens, or go and find the wild pheasants nests and make an assessment. I remember thinking that there would be a lot of pheasants with a long life ahead, as there would be very little shooting for some time to come. Poachers would take advantage, no doubt, but for the moment, I was really getting all the enjoyment of the Norfolk countryside.

I was expecting another visit from Sir Max Pemberton, as a recent letter informed me:

***Dear Chinnock,***

***I hope you have cured the invalids and that all are well at Stody now. Lady Pemberton and I thought it would be better not to throw extra burdens on you and the staff while you have sickness in the house so we have put off our return until we have better news from you. I have been very busy with the newspapers, so it is a good thing I was here. I now propose to return to you in about a fortnight, but only if you are all well again. Could you in the meantime be good enough to let me have some sugar and butter? What is Mr Clark's address in London? I hope Colin Brooks is better. My best remembrances to the ladies, please.***

***Yours sincerely,***
***Max Pemberton***

Viscount Rothermere had, before the outbreak of hostilities, sent on loan to an exhibition in Budapest, eight very valuable pictures. It was now assumed that they would be lost for the duration of the war, at least. This information was passed on to me in a recent communication from Mr Herbert Cescinsky, who was naturally very concerned.

At this time, all sorts of problems were arising. His Lordship had sent me instructions to arrange to have our food stores, including the Fortnum & Mason stocks which we had built up over the past year, got ready for collection, as he had decided to donate it all entirely to the hospitals, and getting that instruction organised was a considerable task for all the staff, though undertaken quite happily in the knowledge that we were furthering a most generous gesture.

ꟿ

**THE LAST TIME** that I ever had a conversation with Viscount Rothermere was a month before the capitulation of France to Germany, and the reason I recall it so vividly was that he had asked me to accompany him on a stroll in the garden. He enquired after my wife and asked was the new baby expected in September, and what did I think I would do. I said I rather thought I would like to join the R.A.F. "Oh no, that's not the future for you my boy." he said, "You have a wife and family to consider, and what the R.A.F. needs is young and daring personnel – it will be the front line you know! I would advise you to think rather of the Army, as at 28 years of age you wouldn't be young enough to fly."

At about this stage he stopped and took a seat on an oak bench and as I stood, he motioned me to take a seat beside him. "What do you think of the war situation?" he next asked. So I talked of an expeditionary force and several other topics.

"Where do you get such ideas from my boy?"

"From the newspapers My Lord."

"You don't mean to tell me that you believe everything you read in the press?" – and this with a meaningful look. He listened to me for a while and then said, "Chinnock, I'll tell you this, but in the strictest confidence mind you, France will capitulate within a month." It did, and almost to the day – so how could I forget such an amazing prediction. He then went on to say, "How would you like a commission in the Army?" – I didn't know – "I'll get you one if you wish." – I was at a loss.

"I doubt whether my education would come up to expectations."

"That's rubbish my boy, but think it over, I'll buy you a commission, or if you think you would rather be a batman to General Spieres *(sic)*, who is at this moment serving in the Middle East, I'll give you a letter of introduction, but don't worry about a thing, Chinnock, I'll keep in touch. I'll make your wife Rose an allowance of £6 per week for the duration of the war."

"Oh, thank you very much indeed, My Lord."

"Just take matters as they come." he told me, "Just wait for your call-up in the army. I shall be going to America to help speed up the aircraft production on behalf of Lord Beaverbrook, the Air Minister. It's quite possible that I may never see you again. You may live to see the end of this dreadful war but I don't think I shall." This was another true prediction, for it came to pass.

Our war talk over, we changed the subject, and as we reached the terrace I took my leave of him, and went at once in search of my wife to tell her the good news. It was a most comforting thought that she would be receiving £6 per week for the duration of the war. She was by now well into her pregnancy, so she was happy with such an assurance, as for myself, well, I was overjoyed.

Not long after this time there was a national appeal by the Air Ministry for aluminium, and needless to say, every aluminium pot and pan was swiftly dispatched to swell the growing needs of the country, so perhaps it was as well that we possessed an enormous amount of copper utensils that would tide us over the immediate requirements.

Eric Wakefield, my first footman, as well as Leonard Green and Stanley Walpole, the two under-footmen and myself, had received our call-up papers by this time, so that good-byes were imminent. Eric Wakefield was the first to go and soon afterwards Leonard and Stanley. Stanley Walpole married one of our housemaids quite suddenly. There were at that time lots of young people marrying their sweethearts before taking up their military service.

My call-up papers arrived in June, and not wanting to leave my wife three months before our baby was due, I applied for a postponement certificate and appeared before a Military Service (Hardship) Committee on the 3rd July 1940 and my stay of liability for service was granted. So it was nice to be able to return from Norwich with news for my wife that I would be with her when our baby was born.

About this time, the full truth was becoming quite evident; Stody was to be handed over to the Military Authorities. The Ladies Wilson were still with us, and we were entertaining some serving officers and other ranks, a whole platoon in fact, were in the gardens.

Mrs Adelaide Wilson had asked if it would be in order for the lads to make use of the swimming pool, and having the officers' consent, the other ranks were most eager to take advantage. We were, therefore, in business again. Sandwiches and beer were soon available and as the ladies entertained the officers, I took delight in looking after the other ranks. Quite a few were by now splashing about in the pool and obviously enjoying themselves immensely. Others taking their ease and enjoying the free cigarettes and beer and doing justice to the sandwiches which we had placed around on glass-topped table furniture that we used in the gardens.

They were the Royal Army Medical Corps and would be part of the Unit that would be taking over Stody in due course, and they spent a carefree couple of hours with us before taking their leave and all seemed to have enjoyed their experience.

Within the next few days, I had been anticipating news from Herbert Cescinsky and it wasn't long in coming. The ladies had returned to London, and he 'phoned me to be prepared to receive the Pall Mall Depository people. They would be coming to remove all the furnishings and he, himself, would be arriving ahead of them. I was to book him into the Feathers Hotel at Holt. I still had quite a few maids in the house; the ones who lived in the locality were the ones who stayed until the end. They could hardly believe this was really taking place, nothing would be the same again, their world was upside down.

Mr Herbert Cescinsky arrived, and, on the morrow, four large vans from the Pall Mall Depository were parked in the drive. In no time at all, with the very experienced staff under the guidance and instructions of this gentleman, the first pantechnicon started to be loaded, the depository foreman and Mr Cescinsky walking around the house and constantly comparing notes. So gradually, the house began to loose its treasures. The work continued until lunchtime, when sandwiches and beer and other refreshments were organised by some of the girls, and these were very much appreciated by the workers.

I was to receive just one more letter from Sir Max Pemberton, which was dated 6th May 1940, and was as follows:

*Dear Chinnock*
*Thank you for writing, you must have had bother and expense looking after my luggage, so will you kindly accept this cheque for £5 just as a temporary recognition of your recent bother with my baggage.*
*I hope to be at Brancaster in June if things don't get impossible here. I shall make an effort then to get over and thank you and the staff for all your kind attention when I was with you.*
*I don't think they should call upon you for service. You have a responsible position which should protect you.*
*Meanwhile we in London are rather on the gloomy side. Mr Colin Brooks lunches with me next Friday so I may then have some Norfolk news.*
*We join in sending you all our good wishes.*
*Yours,*
*Max Pemberton*

I was neither to see him or hear from him again. He was an elderly gentleman in 1940 and I suspect he never survived the horrors of war years, and I felt that I had lost a personal friend. He had been a close friend and companion of Lord Northcliffe and would often reminisce with me. He it was who told me that the *Daily Mail* was one of Northcliffe's greatest journalistic achievements, and that the home of the *Daily Mail* came to be known as Northcliffe House, and that the home of the *Daily Mirror* came to be known as Geraldine House after the mother of the Harmsworths, Geraldine Mary. I consider myself lucky indeed to have had the fortune to have met and talked with people of this calibre.

It was then that I had the opportunity to talk with Mr Cescinsky, whilst we had a private drink and a few sandwiches. He wasn't relishing his job, that was obvious, and it was very sad for all concerned. He enquired after my wife's health and was interested to know that we were expecting my call-up, and I was able to tell him I was exempt until sometime in November and that I had received a postponement certificate to that effect. He asked me why I didn't join the R.A.M.C. as he thought I would be invaluable to them at Stody and I would be near my wife at the same time. He said he could see no reason why that couldn't be arranged and that he would draft a letter when he returned to London.

We talked about the same subject on several occasions in between the packing and consulting the house inventory, and I could only think how nice it was of him to be so concerned for my future. Later on, he came to our cottage and met my wife and my daughter, Hilary, who was then just two years old and had very winning ways. He said to us that the Army wouldn't need to take our cottage over and we could be quite comfortable there for some time to come. After a few days the house was at last completely cleared and Mr Cescinsky arranged for the carpenters to come in and board up the staircase and the Adam fireplaces, and so leave everything in order for the taking over by the Military authorities.

The staff had all gone by this time, which left just my own little family in the Gate Lodge, and Miss Kathleen Ponting, our head housemaid, who would stay with us a while and be with my wife when our new baby arrived.

In the meantime, on August 14th, I received the following memorandum from Herbert Cescinsky:

*I have reason to believe that the latest Rolls, EYV 220 is still licensed, but I don't want to trust to people's recollections, so will you please go to the garage and look for the licence holder on the windscreen and see if the 1940 licence is still there. If it is not there, can you ask Higgs if he has taken it out and is still holding it? Don't trust to anyone else about this, but do it yourself and then I will know it is done. A postcard from you will be enough. Why is the small insurance certificate here? Parker handed it to me this morning; this should be carried on the car and should never leave it. Please explain. H.C.*

There was still staff living at the garage, Mr Joe Higgs and his wife were staying there for the time being. Also the estate manager's house was still occupied. The gamekeepers' accommodation and all the gardeners' houses on the estate were still occupied as the Army would not be taking any of these buildings over. Unfortunately, for me, however, it seemed the Army had made known that they might have to ask me to move out, but for the moment, they were understanding in as much as they must give me the opportunity of securing suitable habitation elsewhere.

Then the following letter reached me on 21st August:

*46 Hanover Gate Mansions*
*London N.W.1.*

*Dear Chinnock,*
*Enclosed is the copy of the letter I sent to Clark for signature. Keep this to yourself and know nothing about it, but if Clark won't sign (he may have reasons) when the time draws close, send me this copy back (it is the only one I have) and I will try to get a signature elsewhere, I may even sign it myself. You can jog Clark's memory, but know nothing about the letter itself. Dornoch looks like following Stody (This is for your private ear). What a game! I am leaving the car licences to Clark, it is his funeral.*

*Yours sincerely,*
*Herbert Cescinsky*

What follows now is a copy of the letter in question dated 12th August 1940.

*The Recruiting Officer*
*Norfolk.*

*Wilfred George Chinnock H.R.464*

*Sir,*

*My house, Stody Lodge, Melton Constable, has been taken over by the R.A.M.C. as C.C.S (Casualty Clearing Station) and I have had all the contents removed with the exception of the kitchen requisites, frigidaire, etc, which have been left for the convenience of the occupying units. Stody is a complicated house especially as regards the heating which is on the ceiling-panel system. Chinnock (as above) has been in my employ as steward-butler and understands the working of the house thoroughly but he has been called up for late September. I would like to make the request that if he can be attached to the R.A.M.C. and the Unit occupying Stody, he would be invaluable if any working difficulties were to arise. Chinnock, married and with a small child, occupies the Gate Lodge which has not been taken over, and he has my authority to get into touch with my people in London and to see that any necessary work or service is carried out. If drafted elsewhere, such assistance would not be available for obvious reasons. No-one on the estate understands the working of the house like Chinnock.*

*Yours truly,*
*pp Viscount Rothermere*
*Private Secretary.*

*P.S. This letter has been signed with Lord Rothermere's authority, he being in America.*

By this time, the Commanding Officer had approached me and had explained that he was very sorry to have to say that I must vacate the Gate Lodge at an early date. I explained that I would need to make arrangements as my wife was expecting her baby at any time now, and that I must have time to solve our problems, and so he agreed that we could stay put until after my wife's confinement. This gave me a breathing space to be able to look for accommodation. Mr Clark was staying at his house in Hunworth so I often came into contact with him, and of course, was keeping my communicating with Herbert Cescinsky a close secret, and awaiting events.

In the meantime, there was the question of my Remington repeater rifle, about which I had made arrangements. So whilst in Holt, making enquiries and visiting a few tradespeople and tying up a few queries regarding outstanding accounts, I called in to see the superintendent of police and asked if it would be possible for the firearm certificate for my rifle to be transferred to Mr F.J.Clark's custody. He said that it could be arranged and so I had found a home for it, and I knew that Jimmy Clark would be pleased to take possession. So, on an afternoon shortly afterwards, I went shooting for the last time on the estate with my Remington, and purposely finished my tour close to where I would be handing it over eventually, and made my way to Mr Clark's house in Hunworth. I gave it to him with my blessing and told him that I would let him have the pull-through and a couple of boxes of .22 ammunition the following day. He had not mentioned the letter so I thought that maybe he could have his reasons, or was delaying tactics for the time being, but I didn't let on that I was aware of any impending developments.

I had to busy myself finding a house to live in. I was about the last of the males eligible for military service in the vicinity and was aware of the feeling that I was looking the odd man out. Kathleen, our head housemaid, was keeping my wife company, as she would very soon be having her child. Kathleen was also keeping an eye on our daughter Hilary, who at 2½ years of age was full of the joys of living and quite a handful at the best of times. Dr Hendric had been attending my wife and had made arrangements for the services of a midwife. In the meantime, I had found a bungalow in Holt and was negotiating with the owners. It was a ramshackle affair with three-quarters of an acre, and a cesspool in the garden, so I thought I would look further for something more to our taste, but look as we may, nothing else seemed to be available, and eventually I took my wife to view the bungalow, in the company of Kathleen, and neither of them were very impressed by what they saw. Time was pressing, however, and I had to act soon, so I arranged to let the owners know one way or another within the following week. I rather liked the garden which was well stocked with fruit trees, Victoria plums, damsons and four or five varieties of apples, not to mention a rather nice onion bed and well-established raspberry canes and strawberries which looked very healthy. There was too much garden, in fact, to have to think about with a war on, it was certainly going to be sadly neglected, but by the end of the week the owners couldn't quite make up their minds whether to leave, and with this stalemate situation, we got on with our search once more.

On the twelfth day of September our second daughter was born. Kathleen had suggested that we get the midwife as my wife thought the time was near and very soon, she arrived and within a short time she told me I must get the doctor as the baby was imminent. Leaving my wife in the capable hands of these two ladies, I hurried across to the telephone which was five minutes away.

After what seemed an age I was talking to Dr Hendric and telling him that our baby was soon to be born. He assured me that he would leave immediately and that he would be with us in fifteen minutes or so. I hurriedly retraced my steps to say that the doctor was on his way, only to be told that the baby had already arrived. The suddenness of the news was a mixture of shock and happiness, and I was relieved when, soon after the doctor arrived, he was able to tell us that everything was perfectly normal and that we had a lovely baby daughter and there was no need for his presence any longer. It was, he said, obvious that everything was under control, so shortly afterwards he took his leave saying he would visit us again in the near future.

Kathleen was busy preparing refreshments for us all. The midwife was still with my wife. Kathleen asked what I would like to eat, but I said who could eat at a time like this, and Kathleen replied that my wife had just asked for a boiled egg and bread and butter, and when after a short while I went to see her, she was sitting up enjoying her lightly boiled egg and bread and butter, whilst Kathleen and the midwife were introducing Hilary to her new baby sister. Kathleen had decided that she would like to stay with our family for an indefinite period and we were more than happy with this arrangement. She would be invaluable to us in the circumstances that existed.

We had yet to find a suitable property and now that the baby had arrived, the military would be once again eager to take our little house away from us. I therefore had to renew my efforts to find something as quickly as possible. Mr Colin Brooke had gone back to London and Mr George Ward Price was thinking of following him in the very near future.

Jimmy Clark was still in residence at his house and I saw him quite frequently, but there was no hint of the existence of the letter drafted by Mr Herbert Cescinsky and awaiting a signature. So the cat and mouse game continued and I was resolved to keep my own council. I was to hear from Herbert Cescinsky on only one more occasion and that was to congratulate me on a 100% plus, for after checking the inventory for Stody Lodge, he told me that several items were not even recorded, one example being a beautiful clock from Cartier's, a crystal hexagonal faced with Roman numerals in diamonds, and he asked me how long I had had it in my custody. I was able to tell him that it had arrived here from Stratten House shortly after my arrival at Stody Lodge.

## Chapter XV

# THE LAST MONTHS

**HOWEVER, 'ONCE MORE INTO THE BREACH',** I must find somewhere to live; that was my most urgent priority and I was simply getting nowhere. Eventually I returned to the bungalow at Holt where we had almost come to terms and I was delighted to find that we could now have the property. The old couple had made up their minds to vacate the premises the following week. So we quickly came to terms, the rental would be twelve shillings per week, and for the duration of the war, therefore, our address would be 'Pax, Hempstead Road, Holt, Norfolk'. I had very mixed feelings, as I was aware that the bungalow was not really our choice, but under the circumstances, we would have to come to grips with it. I returned to my wife and Kathleen to report my success and they expressed the view that it might be alright. It was not what they would have desired, but that we would all have to make the best of our situation. Pax, we all agreed, was a lovely name but it was ironical that I would soon be leaving Pax for war.

Holt is ten miles from Cromer, where can be found a large public school with fine modern buildings, whose trustees are the Worshipful Company of Fishmongers. It was originally a grammar school, founded in 1555 by a gentleman named Sir John Gresham, who was born at Holt, hence 'Gresham's School', a very well known seat of learning, but, like other large establishments, it was taken over by military forces.

However, at this particular time, I had to remove my goods and chattels, and the day arrived when we loaded all our belongings onto transport which I was able to organise, and with very many willing hands, we were soon installed in our new abode. I had been going to and fro with my old Austin 10, taking all manner of bits and bobs, but it so happened, that on that particular day, my road fund licence expired and it was, therefore, the last time I was to drive my dear old car.

On the following day, whilst we were all busy cleaning the bungalow and getting a bit organised, Kathleen suddenly remembered that we had left her bicycle behind at Stody, so I said I would go and fetch it. Remembering that my licence had expired, however, I said I would cycle over. Later that afternoon, therefore, I returned to Stody and finding Kathleen's cycle where she said it would be, I then mounted my bicycle and took the other one by the handlebar and proceeded on my way back to Holt. I reached Hunworth, where I had to dismount to walk up quite a steep hill and having reached the top it was now plain sailing to Holt. So I remounted and continued on my way, riding one cycle and pushing the other.

I was on a decline now and it was getting dusk, when suddenly and without the slightest warning, a great rat ran out of the hedge on my left and into the spokes of my wheel, which threw me violently onto the gravel roadway. It must have knocked me out momentarily, for the next I knew I was laying on the roadway and feeling warm blood when I put my hand to my forehead. I knew then that I must get to the doctor, whose surgery was about a mile away, and feeling much better and having now recovered my senses, I remounted and with care managed to arrive at the doctor's surgery. The sister, when she saw me said, "My dear boy, whatever has happened to you?" – my head evidently looked a bit gory. However, she quickly sponged away the blood from around my right eye then announced that it was not half as bad as it looked, thank goodness. By then, Dr Hendric was on the spot attending to a cut over my right eye, and after a local anaesthetic he inserted two clips and put a temporary bandage around my head and told me to come and see him tomorrow.

Thanking both the doctor and the sister, I took my leave. My thoughts then returned home, they would be wondering why I was so late. Luckily as I arrived at the bungalow, Kathleen came to the door, so putting my finger to my lips as she looked aghast at my condition, I explained quickly that I didn't want my wife to be alarmed, and that it was really not as bad as it looked. I then asked her to go and tell my wife what to expect when she saw me. I was soon able to tell my sympathetic family of my experience. However, it was two days before the bandages were removed and a week before the clips were taken out and to this day, I have the scar above my right eyebrow to remind me of my first house moving.

We settled ourselves in our new surroundings after a while, and now it was drawing close to my calling up date. Nothing had developed regarding my joining the Royal Armed Medical Corps at Stody and no mention of the letter was made, but a few snide remarks mentioning white feathers were made, which immediately put my back up, so I resolved there and then to forget the whole idea, and rather to think of Lord Rothermere's suggestion that he would be keeping in touch, and that I should go when my call-up papers came, and wait for future developments, and so it happened.

I had parked my old Austin 10 beside the bungalow and put supports under the axles and I would sell it at the earliest opportunity.

Eventually my papers arrived and I was to report to Inkerman Barracks, Woking, for no other reason than that I could drive a motor car.

My leave-taking was abrupt. Quite suddenly, it was time to go. One moment I had all the time in the world and the next I was wrenched from my beloved surroundings, but I was aware that what was happening to me was also happening to thousands of other young men, so I accepted the situation with as good a grace as I could muster.

On the seventh day of November 1940, therefore, I reported to Inkerman Barracks and was one of the 26th intake: Driver Chinnock 230652 Royal Army Service Corps, and after the pantomime of being kitted out, which every 'Rooky' knows only too well, the squad which I had joined were told in no uncertain terms that we were in for a month's 'square bashing' and that though we might break our mothers' hearts, to be sure we wouldn't break the sergeant's. We would remember our regimental numbers by heart, it wouldn't be difficult to remember – he would see to that, and "mark my words," he said, "you will never forget your number as long as you live."

And so, in this completely new environment of drill, P.T. and NAAFI breaks, not to mention sore feet, the day of the 28th November 1940 dawned, the day, incidentally, that the bottom of my world dropped out, for upon this day during the morning NAAFI break, I saw a picture of Viscount Rothermere in the *Daily Mirror.* The paper was opposite to me, being read by another soldier. The fact of seeing his picture was not the cause of my concern, as he was frequently featured in the newspapers, but the accompanying wording which unfolded as he read his newspaper.

> ***The death of the Rt Hon Viscount Rothermere, whilst carrying out his mission in the United States at the request of Lord Beaverbrook, took place in Bermuda, at the age of 72 years.***

It was a shock indeed and in the circumstances was to be very far reaching. I would not now be hearing any more from him – the die was cast – and I would be very much on my own. My first reaction was a feeling of great loss. My second, that I was glad my wife was getting her allowance and during the days that followed I checked with my wife to know if the payments were still being made. Happily, they were, that is to say, for the present, but I was to receive another shock a few weeks later, when my wife wrote to tell me that she had had a letter from His Lordship's executors telling her that her allowance from him would cease forthwith. This then was the stark reality, there was absolutely no redress. His death was to be an enormous shock to many people, great and small alike, but there was a terrible war on as well, to be borne by all. The Rt Hon Esmond Harmsworth succeeded his father and became the second Viscount Rothermere.

# Chapter XVI

# EPILOGUE

**IT WAS AROUND THIS TIME** that I received a letter from my wife to say that she had decided that our little dog, Judy, must go. She was very reluctant at the prospect, but due to the fact that Judy was snapping at our new baby daughter, my wife had contacted Mr George Ward Price's sister, who already had three Maltese terriers, and asked if she would take her, and she agreed, my wife explaining that with two small children she found it difficult to cope. So it was arranged for her to be collected, and my wife sadly saw her depart, but knowing that she was going to a good home. With her went her basket and lead, and all her little paraphernalia. I agreed that it probably was a good thing to do as there was strict rationing, and feeding her would have become increasingly difficult as time went on.

As for myself, I found it difficult to come to terms with the events of the past few weeks, so it was just as well, perhaps, that I was kept fully occupied on the barrack square in my strange new world. How long would this great international struggle rage? What would be the outcome? Would I come out of it alive and well? Such were the thoughts that I found myself troubled with. I was comforted that my little family were not in London, and might possibly be safe from the bombs, hidden away, as they were, in Norfolk, and I prayed they might escape the ravages of war.

Later I wrote a letter to the new Lord Rothermere and asked if there was anything he could do to improve my situation.

Here is the reply to my letter which I received on the 28th February 1941:

*Northcliffe House,*
*London E.C.4.*

*Dear Sir,*

*Lord Rothermere received your letter, but has been away for some days, at the moment he does not see how he can help you, but should an opportunity arise he will bear you in mind.*

*Yours faithfully,*

*E.M.Young*
*Private Secretary*

In the meantime, I soldiered on, and in due course, I was the recipient of a weekend pass, with which I was jubilant. I soon found myself once again in Norfolk and in the bosom of my dear ones.

Whilst at home, Miss Ravon contacted me and asked could I go and see her on an urgent matter. I will introduce this lady to my readers and take them back again to Stratten House, Piccadilly, where on a certain day when the above mentioned, a lady secretary to the Viscount Rothermere, received from him a picture, and very valuable I might add, of the Madonna and Child, with which she was delighted and thrilled. She took it to her London flat, later to be removed to a house in Kelling near Holt, in Norfolk where she lived with her mother. I duly arrived at this address and was greeted very cordially by both ladies, who enquired after my wellbeing and, after being offered and accepting a glass of sherry, I was to know the reason for her apprehension. She told me that a representative of Viscount Rothermere's executors had been to collect the picture of the Madonna and Child, and had, in fact, taken possession of it. Next, I was asked if I would be prepared to swear in a court of law, that I had witnessed the fact of Viscount Rothermere giving the picture to her on the occasion aforementioned, at Stratten House. I told her I could do that, but I was afraid that it would be to no avail. I said that as far as I understood the situation, there was very little anyone could do in the circumstances. "But he gave it to me, Chinnock," she said, "didn't he?"

"Yes he did, Miss Ravon," I replied, "and had you had the foresight to have been in touch with Mr Herbert Cescinsky, it could have been a very different story, because all the time that the picture was gracing your wall, he was still paying the insurance on it, and in the eyes of the law, His Lordship was still the owner and it had never left his possession. So my going into any court to testify would be a complete waste of time. It is a great pity that you had not tied up all the legalities to your advantage, by getting in touch with Herbert Cescinsky and having the picture removed from the inventory."

I was indeed very sorry, for it was obviously a great shock to the young lady.

ꕤ

**I NOW FIND** that in writing of myself and the first Viscount Rothermere, I shall have to omit my wartime experiences, as in recounting I feel I could write another book of remembrances. So many things took place – good and bad.

I come now to a letter I received on 10th May 1943:

*Radcliffe & Co.,*
*10 Little College Street,*
*Westminster S.W.1.*

*Dear Sir,*

*Viscount Rothermere – deceased*

***In answer to your letter of the 8th instant, upon investigation of the affairs of the late Lord Rothermere it was found that, after providing for death duties, the estate might not be sufficient to provide for payment in full of all his debts, and his estate is now being administered under the supervision of the High Court of Justice. One result was the stopping of all voluntary allowances made by Lord Rothermere during his lifetime. Another result will be that any legacies bequeathed by his will cannot be paid until all the creditors have been paid in full, which, at the present time, seems to be a very unlikely event.***

*Yours faithfully,*
*Radcliffe & Co.*

For some time now, the press had been full of news items, and Rothermere's missing millions was prominent. I was sure I was completely in the dark, only time would tell. At last, thank God, the war was over and now was the time to pick up the pieces. Always, during the conflict, I told myself that if I ever walked away from it alive, I would never, come what may, grumble about my lot again. I had a hero's welcome at Pax Bungalow on my return from the war, complete with a Union Jack hanging from the wall, and we all made merry. By this time, we had two Land Army girls living with us. They had been good company for my wife during the dark days of war. There were many days of rejoicing and feasting, but though happiness had returned to our lives, I still must find some kind of employment. I was sure I would have great difficulty, as nobody appeared to be organised yet, sufficiently, so soon after the war, and I decided that I must get my priorities right.

I had been six years on active service and was then 34 years of age, and in all those years, I had never had any roots. Surely, I thought, my family must have a home of their own. This was the direction my thoughts were taking me. My immediate need was a job of some kind, but as I was now living in the heart of the Norfolk countryside, I must search further afield. Then, out of the blue, I received the following letter from Mr Colin Brooks, who I learned, was now the editor of *Truth*:

***13th March 1946***

***My dear Chinnock,***

***I was glad to hear that you are now demobilised and that you and Rose and the children are re-united. I wonder if you would write me a letter, the sort of letter I could show to other people, saying what kind of job you are looking for, whether with or without Rose, and giving a brief outline of your past experiences, etc. etc. If you will do this, I will certainly look about and let you know the results.***

***With warmest good wishes to you both,***

***Yours sincerely,***

***Colin Brooks***

I was delighted to hear from our good friend and decided that I would call and see him in the very near future.

I had been toying with the idea of seeing the new Viscount Rothermere, so I 'phoned Warwick House, St James's to find out if that was in order, and found to my delight that he would see me, and I was furnished with a time and a date. So at the appointed time I was in his presence. He had lost none of his charm and was interested to know of my experiences during the war years, and shook me warmly by the hand. He asked me what I was going to do with my future, and my reply was that I planned to raise a mortgage and buy myself a house. He said he couldn't help in that direction, but he could offer me a job. He had recently purchased a property called Daylesford in Gloucestershire, which he was having completely rewired. He said I could, if I liked to, talk to my wife about it.

"By all means think it over." he said, "Leave your address with my butler on your way out."

I thanked him and took my leave and found in the hand that shook mine good-day, a tenner to help me on my way. "It's been nice seeing you again Chinnock" were his parting words.

Earlier on that day, taking advantage of being in London, I had gone to the offices of *Truth* in Queen Anne's Gate and was fortunate enough to catch Mr Colin Brooks in his office. He had been pleased to receive me and asked after my wife and family. We had a very agreeable conversation and indulged in reminiscences of the days gone by. He was most eager to be of some help. We said our good-byes and I was off on my train journey back to Norfolk, to tell my wife of my day's experiences in London. I turned my thoughts to The Hon Vere Harmsworth – I would, I thought, have liked to work for him, but at that time, he was still only just twenty years of age, so to think of approaching him was out of the question, but I did meditate and think of all sorts of situations and possibilities.

After quite a busy day, I was glad to arrive home once again. I had arranged a temporary job at the Grand Hotel, Cromer. They were getting their furnishings from depositories and getting the hotel in readiness for the 1946 season, so I would be occupied for quite some months it transpired. Then on the 29th March I received another communication from Mr Colin Brooks.

*Frith Buildings*
*Carteret Street*
*Queen Anne's Gate,*
*London S.W.1.*

*Dear Chinnock,*

*I was glad to see you today, and to learn that you are now out of the forces. The unexpected death of the late Lord Rothermere in the early months of the war after you joined the forces, may have left you without any reference from him. Please do not hesitate to refer anybody to me, as I will readily testify to your efficiency and courtesy when you were Lord Rothermere's butler in his country house in Norfolk, and to that of Mrs Chinnock when, before your marriage, she managed Lord Rothermere's flat at Stratten Street.*

*Certainly, on the innumerable times when I was His Lordship's guest, you seemed to me to leave nothing undone for the comfort of his household and its smooth running.*

*With good wishes,*
*Colin Brooks*

Mr Colin Brooks was a most charming man and both he and his wife would often take tea with us in our cottage whenever they came to their Norfolk house at Edgefield with their children. We were on quite familiar terms with all of them – a lovely family indeed. It was this gentleman whom Lord Rothermere appointed as his literary legatee and gave him all papers and documents pertaining to himself after his demise, and so he knew that to find another situation I would be extremely lucky to emulate the one that I had enjoyed whilst in Viscount Rothermere's service. I had suggested to my wife that maybe I would have more opportunity as an English butler in America, but after some thought she said that she would rather we stayed in England, and knowing full well myself that, as a country, ours was hard to beat as a desirable place in the world to be, that idea was quickly scotched.

We lived quite happily for a while at Pax in Hempstead Road. The feeling of being free from war was, in itself, a relief and we enjoyed our days together and took advantage of a lovely springtime. It was great to be alive, and one day I received a communication from Lady O'Neill, recently married to the second Viscount Rothermere. She wrote of the situation at the recently acquired Daylesford and asked me to get in touch with her at an early date.

After giving very serious thought to the matter and talking it over with my wife who, of course, as well as myself had known Her Ladyship when she was being entertained at Stody Lodge, we decided to decline her invitation. My priority was still a house of our own, and so I was resolved that we would put the idea of working for the second Viscount from our minds and concentrate our efforts on finding a home of our own.

ഇ

**TO CONCLUDE THIS STORY** I must take my reader to 25th August 1961, just 21 years after the death of the first Viscount Rothermere, when the following communication from his executors reached me:

*Dear Sir,*

*Viscount Rothermere – deceased*

***We are glad to be able to tell you that the executors are now in a position to pay you the balance of the legacy of £156.0s.0d. to which you are entitled under the will of the late Lord Rothermere. You will remember that you have already received £31.4s.0d. on account of your legacy, so the balance amounts to £124.16s.0d. We enclose a form of receipt for this amount which we should be glad if you would sign in the presence of a witness who should add his name, address and occupation. The witness should be a clergyman, Justice of the Peace, bank official or solicitor who knows you personally.***

*Please return the receipt to us when it has been signed, and we will then send you a cheque for the amount of the balance of your legacy.*

*We are, Dear Sir*
*Yours faithfully,*
*Radcliffe & Co.*

Altogether, over the twenty-one years, I had received about twelve communications from Radcliffe & Co. I won't include all the correspondence, but think this one that follows should not be omitted.

*6th March 1957*

*Dear Sir,*

*Viscount Rothermere – deceased*

*Further to our letter of the 1st March, we have now had an opportunity of looking into various points raised by you in your letter. According to the account book which was kept by Mr Clark, you were receiving £3.0s.0d. a week and in these circumstances, you are entitled to a legacy of £156.*

*As you are no doubt aware, the deceased's estate was administered under the control of the Court, as it was believed until quite recently, that the estate would prove to be insolvent and that it would not be possible to pay the deceased's creditors in full. As a result of the careful administration of the estate, the deceased's assets have realised more than sufficient to pay all the creditors in full, and the administration expenses, leaving a surplus, which is available for distribution among the legatees.*

*In addition to the legacies bequeathed to the servants, the deceased also left legacies to other beneficiaries whom we will hereafter refer to as the Principal Legatees, and they have notified us that they agree to the proposal that the legacies bequeathed to the servants, should be paid in full. Before the executors can make payment, however, they require an indemnity to be signed by the principal legatees indemnifying the executors in respect*

*of the payments. The necessary deed of indemnity has to be fully approved by all the principal legatees and signed by them before you can receive your legacy in full. As this may take some time, the executors are making an interim payment of 4/- in the pound in respect of the servants legacies.*
*We enclose a form of receipt for the sum of £31.4s.0d. being a payment of 4/- in the pound on the sum of £156. We shall be glad if you will sign the receipt over a 2d stamp in the presence of a witness, who should sign and add his or her address and occupation. On the return of the receipt, we will forward a cheque for £31.4s.0d.*

*We are, Dear Sir*
*Yours faithfully,*
*Radcliffe & Co.*

ꕥ

**ON LOOKING BACK,** I can only say that my life was greatly enriched just by the fact of having known such a great man. Rothermere was a man in a million, and everyone who worked for him knew, a man of great strength and intellectual brilliance. To say that I have enjoyed very much writing about my life with him, would be an understatement.

I often take my thoughts down memory lane, and on one such day, I wondered what could have happened to the Princess Stephanie Hohenlohe. So I wrote to *Live Letters* of the *Daily Mirror* on the 6th February 1962 and learned the following:

*Dear Mr Chinnock,*
*...........the last information we had regarding Princess Stephanie Hohenlohe was in 1941, when it was reported that the U.S. State Department had issued a warrant for her arrest. She was stated to be a Hungarian associate of Hitler and was allowed to leave London for the United States in 1939.*
*She had been admitted into the United States of America on a*

*visitors permit, but when on 17th December 1939 she asked for an extension, she was ordered to leave the country in four days, but she decided to fight the order.*

*Kind regards.*
*The Editor*
*LIVE LETTERS*

**I HAD ALWAYS THOUGHT, as also had my wife, that we would like to live on the south coast, and so we came to settle in Bognor Regis, where we brought up our two daughters. Yes, we had roots now, and we all thoroughly enjoyed our new-found happiness, in the Sussex countryside. I have always been very interested to follow the fortunes of the Rothermeres, and read in the press of the announcement that to mitigate future death duties, two settlements exceeding £4,500,000 had been made and that in 1971 Esmond, Lord Rothermere, a considerable art collector, had retired after 40 years as Chairman of Associated Newspapers and spent a great deal of his time abroad, and that at that time he was thought to be worth £100 million. We also read that he was seriously ill in a Monte Carlo clinic and later the announcement of his death, and my wife and I were grieved at the news. So now, Vere Harmsworth becomes the third Viscount Rothermere.**

---

**Editor's Note:** Princess Hohenlohe remained in the U.S. while there were several attempts to deport her. The officer in charge of her case was Immigration Service chief, Major Lemuel Schofield. Eventually, she was allowed to stay in the U.S. and there have been several different reasons given for this change of heart. It is on the record that she had an affair with Schofield. However she remained in the U.S. until the end of the war when she returned to Germany. She worked for the media for some years and died in 1972.